W. B. YEATS
and his world

W.B. YEATS

and his world

BY MICHEÁL MAC LIAMMÓIR
AND EAVAN BOLAND

 THAMES AND HUDSON · LONDON

Printed in Great Britain by Jarrold & Sons Ltd, Norwich

ISBN 0 500 13033 7

The church and churchyard, Drumcliff, County Sligo

On 13 June 1865, in Sandymount, a seaside suburb of Dublin, William Butler Yeats was born. His ancestors, by his own account, were men and women of personality and of markedly conflicting political persuasions. One of them saved the life of the national hero Patrick Sarsfield during the last turbulent years of the seventeenth century; another, almost a hundred years later, was a sworn friend of Major Sirr, the most committed enemy of Irish self-government. Sirr was the man who in 1803 arrested the rebel leader Robert Emmet, and strongly approved of the death-sentence which was imposed on him. On the other hand, again, Yeats' great-grandfather was an admiring supporter of young Emmet and mourned for his untimely death on the scaffold.

The family of Yeats' father were mercantile settlers, one of whom, a Church of Ireland clergyman, John Yeats, was appointed in 1805 to the living of Drumcliff in County Sligo. The long and close connection of the poet's family with Sligo dates from this event. John Yeats' image was to influence the poet in his choice of a burial site, for in one of the last of his poems he cries:

> *Under bare Ben Bulben's head*
> *In Drumcliff churchyard Yeats is laid.*
> *An ancestor was rector there*
> *Long years ago.*

5

(*Above*) The poet's mother (*née* Susan Pollexfen), by John Butler Yeats

Sligo. St John's Church, in which Yeats' ▶
parents were married, is in the foreground.
The Sligo mountains can be seen in the
background

John Butler Yeats, the poet's father. A
self-portrait

John Yeats' eldest son, William Butler Yeats (the poet's grandfather), also took holy orders, becoming curate in the parish of Moira, County Down, and then (after his marriage to Jane Corbet, of Sandymount, Dublin) rector of the parish of Tully-lish, in the same county. The family association with Sligo was continued by his eldest son, John Butler Yeats, who married Susan Pollexfen of Sligo in St John's Church, Sligo, on 10 September 1853.

It was in fact his mother's family, the sea-faring Pollexfens and Middletons, that exercised the stronger hold on the poet's imagination during his boyhood. In 1833 William Pollexfen – a prosperous shipowner, and the poet's grandfather on his mother's side – had sailed into Sligo in his ship *The Dasher* and married Miss Elizabeth Middleton, a daughter of his widowed cousin. The Middletons were also shipowners, and William in due course became a partner in their firm, which

Jack B. Yeats as a boy, by John Butler Yeats

was to take the name of Pollexfen. William Pollexfen must have been a man of personality, for the memory of him haunted his grandson to the end of his life, and Yeats has told us: 'Even today when I read *King Lear* his image is always before me, and I often wonder if the delight in passionate men in my plays and in my poetry is more than his memory.'

The Pollexfens were talented and had the reputation of being great talkers. The poet has told us that one of the Yeats family – he does not specify who it was – spoke 'the only eulogy that turned my head: we have ideas and no passions, but by marriage with a Pollexfen we have given a tongue to the sea-cliffs'. The Pollexfens were handsome too, and Susan, with her dark hair and oval face and enormous eyes, was thought 'the most beautiful girl in Sligo'. She was in truth a lovely crea-ture, as became a young lady who was to be the wife of a distinguished portrait painter, also the mother of Willie, the greatest of modern Irish poets, and of Jack, the most famous Irish artist of his generation. There was also another son, Robert (who was to die while still a child), and there were two daughters: Susan, known to the family and the family's friends as Lily, and Elizabeth, who was always called Lolly, nicknames of an unexpected frivolity for the daughters and sisters of aesthetes, and curiously inappropriate for the composed and dignified women they became.

Yeats' mother   Their mother, Mrs Susan Yeats, we are told, read few books and had hardly any interest in painting. She never went to an exhibition even of her husband's pictures, or to his studio to see what work was in progress there. But she wrote some exquisite letters to her betrothed in the days of their courtship, telling him of her delight in the tumbling clouds over Sligo Bay, of tales told by the pilots and the fishing people

8

Sir John Poynter, R.A.

of Rosses Point, and of the whispered talk of the servants at the fireside, stories of ghosts and fairies.

One can discern in these letters certain traits and tastes – especially an absorption in the invisible world – which Mrs Yeats, rather than her husband, may have handed on to her eldest son. John Butler Yeats, on the other hand, though he was the son and grandson of rectors of the Church of Ireland, had little interest in anything beyond the visible world. Though it was at first intended that he should enter the Church, he became a barrister; then, after his marriage, he abandoned his legal career to become a professional artist. He probably regarded his eldest son's growing preoccupation with the supernatural world and with mystical theories and phenomena as being relevant enough to a poet's calling, but he himself shared none of the boy's interest in these subjects. It is likely that John Yeats was reacting against a strictly orthodox family tradition of religious belief; this would have been made easy for him by his own warm and easy-going temperament – in contrast to his eldest son's meditative reserve – by his cheerful outlook on life, and by his almost total lack of money sense. As long as there were interesting heads to paint, books to read, people to talk to, and something to eat, what did it matter what might or might not be the order of things beyond the veil between the visible and invisible worlds? The visible was good enough for him, as was right and natural for the painter of men and women. Life was good, and his own exuberant youth had been passed among people whose views on life were probably very similar to his own. After he had decided to follow the career of an artist, he and his family moved in 1868 from Dublin to London, where he studied at Heatherley's Art School, and later under Sir John Poynter at the Academy Schools. Though he was a man of

Yeats' father

9

talent and temperament, he possessed little flair for acquiring popular fashionable appeal, since he painted neither 'problem pictures' on the one hand, nor flattering portraits of society beauties on the other. Moreover, as we have noticed, he lacked any business instinct. It is easy, therefore, to understand why the family was not a wealthy one.

However, as a certain Johnnie McGurk, a Sligo barber, once remarked, 'the Yeatses were always respectable', a phrase treasured by Willie, who had an instinc-

Yeats in 1907, by Augustus John. Though executed at a later phase of the poet's life, this etching is of particular interest at this point of the narrative in view of the horoscope discussed below

George Pollexfen, by John Butler Yeats
And then I think of old George Pollexfen,
In muscular youth well known to Mayo men
For horsemanship at meets or at racecourses.

tive love for respectability, for order, for 'measured ways'. It is impossible to imagine him at his ease among tinkers, in the way of John Millington Synge, or among prostitutes, in the way of Toulouse-Lautrec, and it is characteristic of him that in later years, in the London of the 1890s, his closest friend, apart from Arthur Symons, should have been not Ernest Dowson, not Francis Thompson, nor any other man of undisciplined life, but Lionel Johnson, the quiet, scholarly poet and Roman Catholic convert. Eventually, he half-shunned even Johnson, when Johnson started to drink to excess.

If we consider the poet's life-long faith in astrology it is interesting to recall a horoscope procured for him by his uncle George Pollexfen from a friend who appears not only to have had a considerable knowledge of the ancient art, but who had never met the young Yeats and apparently knew nothing about him. In this horoscope Saturn, it seems, is most in the ascendant; Mercury trine to ascendant; Saturn and Herschel (Uranus) are trine to the moon and Jupiter sextile to the moon. The native's personal characteristics are described as follows:

'Dry and cold, a swarthy complexion, black hair and dark eyes ... the nose is thin, inclined to bend down over the lips, nostrils closed, chin long and rather large ... head held slightly forward ... the native is profound in imagination, reserved, patient, melancholy; in arguing and disputing grave and austere in manner ... a lover of all honest sciences, a searcher into, and delighter in, strange studies and novelties ... subject to see visions and dream dreams.'

This passage gives an uncannily accurate account of Yeats' appearance and character except for the reference to him as 'a lover of all honest sciences', since the poet's disdain for those sciences that are generally accepted as 'honest' was as marked as his lyrical genius. It was the study of those sciences that so easily lend themselves to dishonesty – astrology and spiritism – that held an irresistible fascination for him throughout his life.

Perhaps it was some influence in his stars that accounted for the unhappiness he had felt as a boy. Even when he thought about God his mind was filled with a conviction of his own wickedness. Outwardly, for him, his early days should have held little but memories of happiness; yet, as he has told us in one of his autobiographies, he could recall little of his childhood but its unhappiness. There was no reason for this, for, as he confesses, 'no one was unkind', and his surroundings were consistently agreeable.

Childhood in Dublin and London

The first three years of his infancy were passed in his birthplace, a small, pleasant house called 'Georgeville' at the head of Sandymount Avenue, Dublin. When, in 1868, the family moved to London so that his father could study to become a professional painter, they settled at 23 Fitzroy Road, Regent's Park, which was to be their home until 1874.

'My earliest memory,' the poet has written, 'is of looking out of an Irish window at a wall covered with cracked and falling plaster.' This of course was at Sandymount. Later on he looked out of another window – there was about Yeats, as about so many respectably bred Irishmen, something endearingly old-maidish; he was, it seems, as a child, perpetually peering out of windows – and this time he saw 'some boys playing in a London street'. This was presumably at Regent's Park. But the years in London held but few memories for him in comparison with visits to 'Merville', his grandfather William Pollexfen's house in Sligo, 'so big that there was always room to hide in'. There was a red pony for the little boy at 'Merville', a garden where he could wander, and two dogs who followed him wherever he went. Even though he only visited Sligo on these occasional long

Sligo

holidays, it was Sligo, far more than London (and far more, also, than Dublin, after his family returned there) that coloured the child's thoughts and left there the most enduring images of his life. For Sligo was full of whispered talk of fairies and ghosts, and the boy was all ears. It was in Sligo that he heard a servant telling his mother that she had heard the *Beansí* (pronounced 'Banshee') crying for his young brother Robert on the night before the child's death. He was told, too, though he could not remember it, that he said he saw, in his grandfather's Sligo house, a supernatural bird in a corner of the room.

Sligo, with its quiet, rambling streets, its irregular eighteenth-century houses and churches, its wide harbour set about with ships and quay-sides and framed by sloping fields and bare mountain-tops, was for ever in the background, and very

'Georgeville', 5 Sandymount Avenue,
Dublin. Yeats' birthplace

23 Fitzroy Road, Regent's Park,
London, where the Yeatses lived from
1868 until 1874

13

Glencar lake, with Ben Bulben in the background

in boyhood when with rod and fly,
Or the humbler worm, I climbed Ben Bulben's back
And had the livelong summer day to spend.

The harbour, Sligo

for many a creak gave the creel in the cart
That carried the take to Sligo town to be sold,
When I was a boy with never a crack in my heart.

15

(*Left*) Elizabeth C. Yeats ('Lolly') and Lily (Susan) Yeats, two portraits by John Butler Yeats

often indeed in the foreground, not only of Willie's life but also of the lives of his brother and sisters. Jack, the most profoundly national of Irish painters, felt throughout his life this passion for Sligo. So, in a slightly lesser degree perhaps, did Susan and Elizabeth, both of whom, after many years in England, returned to Dublin to establish the Cuala Press, still renowned for its beautifully illuminated and printed poems and ballads and for its pictures, linen and tapestries.

In 1874, when Willie was nine, the family changed their London address from 23 Fitzroy Road to 14 Edith Villas in West Kensington, and in the following *Schooldays in* year Willie began to attend the Godolphin School in Hammersmith. There he *Hammersmith* displayed an unexpectedly fierce desire for physical prowess. He has told us of his initial terror of plunging into the swimming bath while he stepped down, presumably shuddering, on the ladder until the water reached his thighs. But one day when he was alone he accidentally fell off the springboard, and after that all was well, for he would dive from greater heights than any of the other boys and would pretend not to be out of breath when he emerged after swimming under the

16

The Godolphin School (now Godolphin and Latymer School), Hammersmith, in 1862

water. He would also be careful not to pant or show any signs of strain after running a race. Again, discussing the same period, he tells us how 'often, instead of learning my lesson, I covered the white squares of the chess-board on my little table with pen-and-ink pictures of myself doing all kinds of courageous things'.

The Godolphin School, however, he described as an 'obscene bullying place, where a big boy would hit a small boy in the wind to see him double up, and where certain boys, too young for any emotion of sex, would sing the dirty songs of the street. But I dare say', he continues with charming, impersonal gaiety, 'it suited me better than a better school.' It is in such phrases that one discovers the lovable side of Yeats: a sudden and surprising humility, an uncomplaining acceptance of the drab, inevitable things of life that is akin to the temper of the visionary or of the saint, lining up in the queue with everybody else to receive his share of milk or bread, his tin tray or his earthen bowl in his hand. But Yeats was haughty too, from the beginning to the end. A gaunt unwavering purpose burned in him day and night. His early scorn for what the world accepts as reality drove him, when he was still little more than a boy, not only to romanticism but to the last and most logical refuge of the romantic: to an endless quest for the invisible world and its inhabitants.

Throughout his London schooldays, the boy was incurably lonely for the west of Ireland. The visits to Sligo had become lamentably few, and in his *Reveries over Childhood and Youth* he writes:

'A poignant memory came upon me the other day while I was passing the drinking fountain near Holland Park, for there I and my sister had spoken together of our longing for Sligo and our hatred of London. I know we were both very close to

17

Yeats as a boy, a sketch by
John Butler Yeats

8 Woodstock Road, Bedford Park, ▶
London, where the Yeatses lived
from 1876 until 1880

tears and I remember with wonder, for I had never known anyone that cared for
such mementoes, that I longed for a sod of earth from some field I knew, something
of Sligo to hold in my hand.'

In truth the lanky boy, travelling every day between West Kensington and his
school at Hammersmith, was dreaming incessantly of 'the monsters and marvels'
that haunted the roads between Sligo and Rosses Point. The mood of the Irish
exile – the craving for Sligo, for the intangible magic of its wild, dark earth and
changing skies – followed him everywhere. In 1876 the Yeatses moved from Ken-
Bedford Park sington to one of the new houses at Bedford Park, the first garden suburb. Here the
irregular streets, the red-brick and timber houses and the great trees throwing their
shadows over the roadway gave the young boy a certain aesthetic pleasure. But
still the mood of nostalgia persisted. Even the dancing lessons which Willie, Jack
and their sisters took at the house, where the walls were covered in William

18

Morris wallpaper and 'all the woodwork was painted peacock blue', could not cure the boy of his consciousness of being a stranger in a strange land.

But in 1880, when he was fifteen, the family left London for Ireland and took a *Howth* thatched cottage on top of the cliffs at Howth. Here there were more stories to listen to, for the hills and woods of Howth are fairy-haunted; every corner of the village has its legend and its spectre. The Yeatses employed a servant, a fisherman's wife, who was a mine of local lore and whose accounts of supernatural adventures provided Willie with material for a whole chapter, called 'Village Ghosts', in *Celtic Twilight*, his first published prose work, which was to appear in 1893.

The years spent in Howth were a period of great development for the poet. Every morning he and his father would take the train into Dublin and eat the first meal of their day in John Yeats' studio in York Street close by St Stephen's Green. The father would read poetry aloud over the breakfast-table, verses from *Manfred*, or some great speech from *Coriolanus*, and his son's pleasure in passionate utterance

Erasmus High School, Harcourt Street, Dublin

and noble gesture may well have found its first inspiration in these readings. But after the brief dreamy delight, when the last cup of tea had been drunk, the last poem read and discussed, Willie would go off to the Erasmus High School in Harcourt Street, where it still stands.

At the end of the day, father and son would return to Howth. Often, on summer nights, the boy would steal out of the house after supper to sleep in a cave, with a candle, a tin of cocoa and some biscuits as his companions. He was a restless creature, for ever in quest of some new solitary adventure. Sometimes he would desert his cave and spend the night sleeping among the rhododendrons in the demesne of Howth Castle. It was at Howth, he has said, that the first awakening of sex came to him, although about the manner in which it made itself known he tells us nothing. Probably, like many imaginative egocentrics on the threshold of manhood, he endeavoured to suppress all bodily passion as being too common place, too much shared by every Tom, Dick and Harry to be given any import ance in the design he was planning: a life that was to be dedicated to strange wisdom, magical power. It was in 1882, during this period, that Willie (now at an age when most adolescents are beginning to seek the companionship of girls) made his earliest experiments in verse.

In 1883 the family moved from Howth to 10 Ashfield Terrace, Rathgar, a suburb of Dublin, and a year later the boy left Erasmus High School for the *Art school in* Metropolitan School of Art in Kildare Street, where his father was a master. *Dublin* The son, still in many ways very much of a child, was beginning to be self conscious,

20

Howth

The bay and cliffs, Howth

St Stephen's Green, Dublin

Yeats as a young man

to walk 'with an artificial stride in memory of Hamlet', he tells us, pausing now and then to watch his reflection in a shop window and wishing that the wind would blow his 'long loose tie into a permanent Byronic shape'. The actor's image of himself was becoming more and more important; the image of his heart's desire was growing into a more definite and serious pattern.

At the art school in Kildare Street, in 1884, he first met the young man to whom eventually he was to dedicate his first published volume of poems. The young man seemed a fellow spirit, being the most bewildering and perhaps the most significant figure in the contemporary Irish scene. He came from the North, from the County Armagh; his name was George Russell, and he chose to be called AE, the first two letters of the word 'aeon', because he wished always to remain 'impersonal, unknown and obscure'. He could not draw the model, Yeats has told us, as the other students drew it, because some other shape always rose before his eyes. One of these shapes – a vision of St John the Baptist in the desert – impressed itself upon the poet's memory, perhaps because AE, like himself, was normally more preoccupied with pagan than with Christian beliefs. AE saw

AE (George Russell)

23

AE (George Russell)

Yeats, a drawing (1903) by AE

John O'Leary, a photograph taken in 1894 by ▶
T. W. Rolleston. Many years later, Yeats was to write
Romantic Ireland's dead and gone,
It's with O'Leary in the grave.

visions continually, and was already beginning to mould them into verse as he was later to translate them into pictures. A more profoundly natural mystic than Yeats, a more gifted seer, he had less literary genius and, perhaps, less aesthetic taste. According to a description of his poems in *The Celtic Twilight*:

'There were fine passages in all, but these were often embedded in thoughts which have evidently a special value in his mind, but are to others the counters of an unknown coinage. . . . At other times the beauty of the thought was obscured by careless writing as though he had suddenly doubted if writing was not a foolish labour. He had frequently illustrated his verses with drawings, in which an imperfect anatomy did not altogether hide extreme beauty of feeling.'

These are significant words, coming from so young a man in analytical praise of the work of another, even younger man, for already Yeats, the artist, was criticizing

the careless writing and imperfect drawing of one who was clairvoyant rather than fine draughtsman, clairaudiant rather than accomplished recorder. Yet the artist also seems to have perceived that the path AE had travelled was leading him beyond the middle way of the arts. Had the young visionary from the County Armagh already perhaps reached that cross-roads from which, centuries before him, St Francis and some others had climbed?

In 1885 Yeats' verse appeared in print for the first time: two of his poems were published in the *Dublin University Review*, which had been founded towards the end of the previous year. It was in 1885 too that he met John O'Leary, the old Fenian leader, 'the handsomest old man', so the poet has told us, that he ever saw. So great was the influence of the older over the younger man, Yeats writes, that 'from O'Leary's conversation and from the Irish books he lent or gave me has come all I have set my hand to since'.

First poems published

Douglas Hyde,
by John Butler Yeats

In O'Leary's house Yeats met Douglas Hyde and John Taylor. Hyde (who in 1893 was to found the Gaelic League, dedicated to preserving and increasing the use of the Irish language) was to become as significant a figure in the pattern of Ireland's destiny as Yeats himself. John Taylor, a member of the Irish nationalist movement and follower of O'Leary, possessed a gift of oratory which was later to stir James Joyce to boundless admiration and which made on Yeats so deep an impression that Taylor's name, to the end of Yeats' life, was affectionately and even reverently quoted by the poet both in verse and in prose.

Katharine Tynan   It was also in the old Fenian's house that Yeats used regularly to meet Katharine Tynan, the poetess, a gentle, talented woman to whom 'the youthful genius', as she rightly perceived him to be, poured out many of his dreams and all of his hopes. But when he had grown into a mature and dominating personality – major poet, great practitioner of mystical studies, the acknowledged leader of Irish intellectual

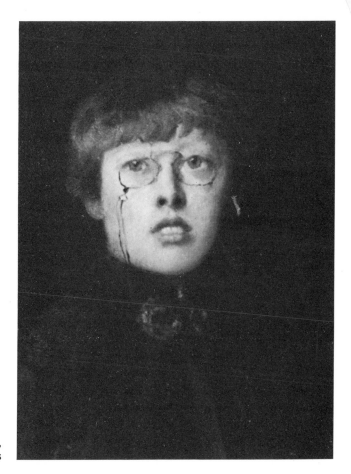

Katharine Tynan,
by John Butler Yeats

energies – estrangement stepped between them. Her affection for him, like that of some adored elder sister, hesitated before what seemed to her a dark and alien mist that gathered about him as a cloud gathers about the head of some well known, well loved mountain. She shuddered at his increasing haughtiness, his deliberate withdrawal from warm, familiar things; she was saddened by what seemed to her his newly acquired snobbery. Above all, it is likely that, however much his interest in the superstitions of the country people may have amused her at first, she recoiled from the increasing sophistication of his experiments in psychical research, from the steady growth of his preoccupation with what, with traditional Catholic disapproval, she must undoubtedly have called 'occultism'.

Ironically, it was Katharine Tynan who brought Yeats to his first séance – possibly in the hope that his passionate inquisitiveness would be cured by some homoeopathic method. The experience was unnerving for them both, for, after

Eardley Crescent, Earl's Court, London.
No. 58, where the Yeatses lived in 1887, is
the house on the left

3 Blenheim Road, Bedford Park, London,
the house which the Yeatses took in 1888

28

Madame Blavatsky

some chilling preliminaries, swiftly followed by a few alarming words (accompanied by actions) from the medium, Miss Tynan left the table and sank to her knees in prayer in a corner, while Yeats, who had been compelled by some unseen force to bang his neighbour's knuckles on the table, then proceeded to break the table. After that he felt that he was going into a trance, then decided that he was not, and finally, unable to remember a prayer, started to recite the opening of *Paradise Lost*. He then began to sense the presence of something 'very evil' in the room.

But in his case, the truth of Wilde's inverted proverb, 'a burnt child loves the fire', seems to have been proved by the events which followed. In 1886 the youth abandoned his artistic studies at the Metropolitan School of Art in order to pursue a literary career. Then, in 1887, a year or so after the adventure at the séance, the Yeats family once more left Dublin for London, where they lived first at 58 Eardley Crescent, Earls Court, and later at 3 Blenheim Road, Bedford Park, where Yeats met the magician McGregor Mathers and also Madame Blavatsky, the founder of the Theosophical Society. Yeats joined the Blavatsky Lodge of the Theosophical Society in London, and in the formidable company of McGregor Mathers and

Madame Blavatsky the exploration of mystical phenomena became for a time an obsession with him and indeed might be said to have influenced well-nigh every subsequent action of his life. Certainly it became the leading force in his writing, and although his days and nights teemed with a hundred other interests, the quest for the unknown was to remain the changeless background.

Abandons art for a
literary career

Yeats' literary activities now began to gather momentum. In 1886 his first dramatic poem, *Mosada*, had been published in Dublin. Now, in 1887, his verse was published in England for the first time, when a poem of his, 'The Madness of King Goll' (see page 34), appeared in the magazine *The Leisure Hour*. In the same year he edited an anthology of poetry which was published in Dublin under the title *Poems and Ballads of Young Ireland*. In 1888 he compiled a volume, entitled

George Bernard Shaw in about 1890   Oscar Wilde in 1894

◀ (*Left*) The living room of Madame Blavatsky's house in Lansdowne Road, London

Fairy and Folk Tales of the Irish Peasantry, which was published in London. His circle of readers grew steadily wider; he was beginning to be accepted by a growing body of opinion as an authority on Irish folk lore and a poet of importance. He made the acquaintance of G. B. Shaw and Oscar Wilde; he also met William Morris and W. E. Henley, and attended many gatherings in their houses.

Throughout this time he continued to return whenever possible, for short or long periods, to Sligo, where he found in his uncle, George Pollexfen, a support for his own studies and beliefs.

After the day's work, uncle and nephew would walk by the sea at Rosses Point – Uncle George on the cliffs or the sandhills, his nephew by the shore – and through a system of cabalistic symbols, taught by McGregor Mathers to the poet, they

The poet and critic W. E. Henley   William Morris, a sketch by John Butler Yeats

would experiment by endeavouring to pass unspoken thoughts and images to and from each other.

In the house there was a servant girl called Mary Battle, who had been in George Pollexfen's service for many years and had what is known in Ireland as 'the sight'. She was a genuine, quite untrained seer, and it was her visions and dreams which had originally aroused George Pollexfen's interest in hidden things. Yeats wrote down everything he learned from Mary Battle, and her visions inspired some of the most impressively simple passages in his works.

'The Wanderings of Oisin'

In George Pollexfen's house, in 1888, he completed a long narrative poem on a theme from Irish legend: *The Wanderings of Oisin*. During the following year, with the aid of John O'Leary and other private subscribers, he published this poem, together with a collection of lyrics and ballads, in a volume entitled *The Wanderings of Oisin and Other Poems*. The lyrics and ballads in this, Yeats' first published book of verse, were in due course reprinted under the title *Crossways*.

The subject matter of the first eight lyrics and ballads in this book grew out of youthful Indian and Arcadian imaginings. Gods and goddesses, princes and priestesses, temples, peacocks and sacred lotus flowers all appear in these pages together with sad and happy shepherds, cloaks of sorrow and poppies on the

32

Rosses Point, County Sligo. Ben Bulben can be seen in the background

Where the wave of moonlight glosses
The dim grey sands with light,
Far off by furthest Rosses
We foot it all the night.

brow: in short, all the pleasant colours and forms of conventional nineteenth-century romanticism. But there is something more besides: a sense of loneliness, of mystery, of a passionate search for some undiscoverable truth, perhaps for some half-remembered wisdom. There is a remarkable precocity of perception in these eight poems; they are filled with a curious sense of weariness, of finality, and, in one of them at least, of loss. But in the last eight poems (there are sixteen in all), Yeats abandons the images of Indian and Arcadian mythology, and the manner of the Pre-Raphaelite school, and turns to Ireland for his inspiration. The younger, more joyous element which pervades these poems was prompted perhaps by the poet's rapturous discovery of his own country as the new, and henceforth permanent, temple of his muse.

Style of early poetry

Any English-speaking romantic with a slight gift might have written lines such as these in 'The Song of the Happy Shepherd':

> *I must be gone: there is a grave*
> *Where daffodil and lily wave.*

The lyrical talent is plain in such lines, but any very young man with a copy of Wordsworth in his pocket and a taste of honey on his tongue might have written

33

them. Again, any young English poet might have written such verses as the following (from 'Anashuya and Vijaya'), for all their eager promise of greater things to come:

> I loved another; now I love no other.
> Among the mouldering of ancient woods
> You live, and on the village border she,
> With her old father the blind wood-cutter;
> I saw her standing in her door but now.

But only Yeats could have written 'The Madness of King Goll' (first published in the magazine *The Leisure Hour* in 1887), which ends with these lines:

> I sang how, when day's toil is done,
> Orchil shakes out her long dark hair
> That hides away the dying sun
> And sheds faint odours through the air:
> When my hand passed from wire to wire
> It quenched, with sound like falling dew,
> The whirling and the wandering fire;
> But lift a mournful ulalu,
> For the kind wires are torn and still,
> And I must wander wood and hill
> Through summer's heat and winter's cold.
> They will not hush, the leaves a-flutter round me, the beech leaves old.

Nor could any poet whose imagination was not on fire with the living legends of his own countryside have written 'The Stolen Child', in which the voice of an earth spirit is heard luring a child from suffering human existence to lands of invisible enchantment:

> Away with us he's going,
> The solemn-eyed.
> He'll hear no more the lowing
> Of the calves on the warm hillside
> Or the kettle on the hob
> Sing peace into his breast,
> Or see the brown mice bob
> Round and round the oatmeal-chest.
> For he comes, the human child,
> To the waters and the wild
> With a faery, hand in hand,
> From a world more full of weeping than he can understand.

34

Glencar waterfall, County Sligo   *Where the wandering water gushes*
From the hills above Glen-Car,
In pools among the rushes
That scarce could bathe a star.

Edward Dowden, the critic and Shakespearian scholar

Cartoon published in the Dublin *Evening Telegraph* in 1889, satirizing the Coercion Act: a repressive measure, passed by the British Government in 1881, which was bitterly resented by the Irish. Gladstone (seen through the bars of the window), who strove for so long to achieve Home Rule for Ireland, is represented as the nation's friend ▶

The thought and the manner are deliberate, cerebral, and highly individual. On the other hand the material, the inspiration, and the imagery of these poems – and of *The Wanderings of Oisin* – come not from this school or that, but from some source beyond the poet's ego, or taste, or early reading: they come from his blood, his senses, his heart. They come, in fact, from his own country, from Ireland herself. The airs that blow over her mountains and the waters that flow through her glens, and the thorn-trees that grow over her haunted burial-mounds become, after centuries of silence, articulate once more, though they speak in the strange new English tongue, through the poet's lips.

The Wanderings of Oisin and Other Poems was, on the whole, well received in both Dublin and London. Critics as diverse as Edward Dowden and Katharine Tynan praised it in Ireland; W. E. Henley and William Morris in England. Yeats was at once eager and vulnerable about the reception of the book, and much of his correspondence at the beginning of 1889 is concerned with the laudatory or hostile attitude of reviewers, the preference of his friends for one poem or another, the progress of sales. His letters at this time have a slightly breathless quality, a new tone of excitement. On 8 March 1889 he wrote to Katharine Tynan:

My dear Miss Tynan,
I got the first substantial gain from my book yesterday. The editor of *Leisure Hour* sent five pounds as an intalment for an article of mine which he has been trying to make his mind up about for a year, at the same time writing to me about Oisin 'every word, every line is alive'.

Maud Gonne   One day in 1889, not long after the publication of *The Wanderings of Oisin and Other Poems*, a certain Miss Maud Gonne called at the house in Bedford Park, bringing with her a letter of introduction from John O'Leary to John Butler Yeats. The poet

Yeats was now in his early twenties, having passed that age when, as he tells us, 'at seventeen years old I was already an old-fashioned brass cannon full of shot, and nothing had kept me from going off but a doubt as to my capacity to shoot straight'. That capacity seemed suddenly to be in jeopardy for all time once he had set eyes on the being who alighted from the hansom and knocked at his father's front door on that fatal spring day. It must have been springtime, because the poet later remembered the apple tree in the garden where the sunlight fell, and how the face of the strange girl standing by the window had the same transparent quality as the blossoming boughs behind her head. She spoke to Yeats and his father of war and of the glories of war, praising it for its own sake, annoying John Yeats by her youthful violence and bewildering his son with her beauty, her height and grace, her pale, luminous complexion, her red-gold hair, her mysteriously angry eyes that seemed golden too, her red lips, her eloquence, and her passion for Ireland's political freedom. From the moment of their meeting all life for Yeats was 'changed, changed utterly'. It was only the demon of an incredible will-power within him that saved him from being entirely wrecked by her; the capacity 'to shoot straight' might otherwise have been lost for ever.

For Maud Gonne did not return his passion. She accepted him with delight as a friend, but she would respond to no love-making. Obsessed by a burning desire to free Ireland from its seven hundred years' domination by England, fanatical to an extent only found among those who react not merely against tyranny but also against a family background that had its share in that tyranny's tradition – for

37

her father was a colonel in the British army and her mother an English lady – she saw in Yeats simply a perfect weapon to be used in the great battle. The love-poems wrung from him by her refusal to become either wife or mistress had no interest for her: she cared only for the element in his poetry which was dedicated to Ireland, and had she had her way he would have become a writer of versified nationalist propaganda, a sort of *fin de siècle* Thomas Davis.

As it was, Yeats allowed Maud Gonne to involve him in many of her political activities. Frustrated passion for a time made him her slave, an easy role for him to assume, for there was much, even in the revolutionary side of her temperament, that delighted him. Like himself, she was fascinated by the supernatural, by dreams and symbols and omens, and all these things were linked in her mind to Irish destinies. Whenever she travelled (and she made many missionary journeys between Dublin and London and Paris) she would be accompanied by dogs and by birds of all kinds: parrots, finches, canaries, and, once, a hawk from Donegal. Yeats, writing of her at this time, alludes to the significance of these birds:

'A nation in crisis becomes almost like a single mind, or rather like those minds . . . that become channels for parallel streams of thought, each stream taking the colour of the mind it flows through. . . . I was sedentary and thoughtful; but Maud Gonne was not sedentary, and I noticed that before some great events she did not think but became exceedingly superstitious. . . . Once upon the eve of some demonstration, I found her with many caged larks and finches which she was about to set free.'

This was not the only occasion, she has explained, on which she practised this superstitious rite. To her, the birds (first caged, and then released) were magical symbols of slavery and liberty. During the 1890s, and for a few years in the early 1900s, wherever she went in Ireland the people gathered to see her pass: her beauty and her patriotic passion had made her the nation's last great romantic heroine. There were many among the poor who believed that her prayer, her touch, her mere presence, had the power to save them from sickness and from the brink of death.

Meanwhile, whether at his writing-table or on some lecture platform, Yeats continued in his endeavour to merge his two greatest passions – 'love of country and love of the Unseen Life', as he had phrased it – to weave them together into a complete philosophy in which they would lie in peace and happiness side by side. But as the country he loved was his own country, and as her accepted faith was of a very different nature from his own, the task was not a simple one. Perhaps he was thinking of this when, many years later, he wrote:

> *The fascination of what's difficult*
> *Has dried the sap out of my veins, and rent*
> *Spontaneous joy and natural content*
> *Out of my heart.*

Maud Gonne as a young woman, by Sarah Purser.

Time can but make her beauty over again:
Because of that great nobleness of hers
The fire that stirs about her, when she stirs,
Burns but more clearly.

Ernest Rhys

Fleet Street, London, in about 1900. The
Cheshire Cheese inn, where the members of
the Rhymers' Club held their meetings,
can be seen on the left
We were the last romantics – chose for theme
Traditional sanctity and loveliness.

Or was it, as some other lines in the poem suggest, of his involvement with the
theatre (which began in the late 1890s) that he was thinking? Or of Maud Gonne,
the most fascinating and most difficult of all human beings who crossed his path?
Or of all these things that wound their threads about him in such confusion that a
man as gifted as he, but with less resolution of will, might well have faltered in
listless despair before the labour of his dedication?

Far from faltering, Yeats was taking an increasingly active part in the literary life
of London. In 1890 he wrote to Ernest Rhys (who had asked him to compile a
set of Irish fairy tales), 'I am growing jealous of other poets, and we will all grow
jealous of each other unless we know each other and feel a share in each other's
triumph'. With the co-operation of a number of friends, Yeats soon translated his
The Rhymers' idea into reality, and in 1891 the Rhymers' Club was formed, Yeats, Ernest Rhys
Club and the scholar T. W. Rolleston being the chief founder members. The Club's

40

T. W. Rolleston, scholar in the Gaelic and German literatures

meetings (held in an upper room of the Cheshire Cheese inn, Fleet Street) were crowded by the younger members of what might be called the 'Post Pre-Raphae-lite' school of literature – a group regarded with faint suspicion by many people, since it seemed to them to represent the bridge between romanticism and decadence.

In some ways the Club was a disappointment: these novel and interesting rhymers were not always novel or interesting talkers. Yeats himself was one of the few members ever to introduce any vital topic, and in later years he recalled how 'conversation constantly dwindled into "Do you like So and So's last book?" "No, I prefer the one before it!"' Yet the other members of the Rhymers' Club had much in common with the Irish poet: a hatred of arid, intellectual verse, and of cut-and-dried philosophies; also a passion for the melody and sense of mystery of which Yeats was already becoming a master. Led to a great extent by him, they

Yeats, a photograph taken by T. W. Rolleston in 1894

'Some Persons of the 90s', a cartoon drawn by Sir Max Beerbohm in 1925. From left to right:
Richard Le Gallienne, W. R. Sickert, Arthur Symons, George Moore, John Davidson,
A. Harlacos, Charles Conder, Oscar Wilde, Sir William Rothenstein, Sir Max Beerbohm,
Yeats, Aubrey Beardsley

turned with enthusiastic seriousness to symbolism, and developed a manner, both in verse and in prose, whose father, whether acknowledged or not, was Walter Pater, and whose mother was a nameless cloudy goddess. The influence of this literary parentage led, at times, to a certain lofty vagueness of utterance. The reader feels that he is present at the performance of a deliberately obscure rite achieved with elaborate whimsicality: the equivalent, in literature, of Art Nouveau in the visual arts.

It was the personalities, however, rather than their philosophies, which remained with Yeats as the bequest of the Rhymers' Club. There on a few rare occasions he would encounter Oscar Wilde, who had always befriended him and whom he afterwards championed; Ernest Dowson, the delicate English lyric poet; John Davidson, the brilliant and melancholy Scot; and, one of Yeats' closest friends during this period, Lionel Johnson. Sadly, despite the formal, classical austerity of his mind and his verse, Johnson began to drink excessively, until at last (as Yeats recalls in *The Tragic Generation*) 'one called to find his outer door shut, the milk on the doorstep sour'. The friendship with Johnson cooled in consequence. And yet Johnson's boyish and tragic image, together with the images of the other Rhymers, haunted the Irish poet's imagination until, in a poem called 'The Grey Rock', published in 1914, he finally articulated his love for them:

> *You had to face your ends when young –*
> *'Twas wine or women, or some curse –*
> *But never made a poorer song*
> *That you might have a heavier purse,*
> *Nor gave loud service to a cause*
> *That you might have a troop of friends.*
> *You kept the Muses' sterner laws,*
> *And unrepenting faced your ends.*

In 1891 Yeats founded, in London, the Irish Literary Society. During the year he returned to Ireland on a visit, in the course of which he asked Maud Gonne to marry him. She refused, but begged him for his friendship. In that year, his mind still obsessed by thoughts of her and of her own obsession to deliver the Irish people from bondage, he wrote a play, *The Countess Cathleen*, whose heroine he moulded in the image of his beloved: Cathleen is a beautiful noblewoman who, having sold her soul to the Devil so that her people may be saved from starvation, eventually goes to Heaven. The production of this play, which did not take place until 1899, was to be attended by much religious and political controversy.

'The Countess Cathleen'

Maud Gonne was all the while absorbed in meetings, demonstrations, elections and other public and secret activities of a 'subversive nature', that frequently took her to London and Paris and to various provincial Irish towns. She adored the

excitement and the danger, and she seemed at one period to have had dreams of a
martyr's death. In many of his later poems, Yeats recalled her as she was at this time.

> *She lived in storm and strife,*
> *Her soul had such desire*
> *For what proud death may bring*
> *That it could not endure*
> *The common good of life.*

She induced him to march with her in one or two demonstrations in Dublin. He
obeyed, walking, as it was reported, 'like one in a dream' at her side. There were the
usual speeches, slogans and cat-calls, a few broken heads, and on one occasion an
ear-splitting accompaniment of shattered window-panes. Through it all she walked,
her golden eyes ablaze, her heart beating fast, 'her laughing head thrown back',

> *Pallas Athene in that straight back and arrogant head.*

Maud Gonne

*The lineaments, a heart that
  laughter has made sweet,
These, these remain, but I
  record what's gone. A crowd
Will gather, and not know
  it walks the very street
Whereon a thing once walked
  that seemed a burning cloud.*

She was in her element; he, floundering like a fish out of water, continued to worship.

*What could have made her peaceful with a mind
That nobleness made simple as a fire,
With beauty like a tightened bow, a kind
That is not natural in an age like this,
Being high and solitary and most stern?
Why, what could she have done, being what she is?
Was there another Troy for her to burn?*

On 11 October 1891 Charles Stewart Parnell died. His rapid ascent to the House of Commons had won over the people to his side; his love-affair with and subsequent marriage to Kitty O'Shea, who was a divorcée, had routed popular Irish hopes of his leadership (Catholic Ireland was still in the main sternly Puritanical)

Charles Stewart Parnell
*He fought the might of England
And saved the Irish poor.*

Kitty O'Shea at about the time of
her marriage to Parnell in June
1891

and alienated the conformist majority. After the death of this ardent patriot and once
beloved man, Yeats, who had been distressed and repelled by the uproar in Irish
political circles caused by the downfall of the great leader, diverted his own
nationalist passions into channels unconnected with parliamentary intrigue. His
tragic love for Maud Gonne still possessed him, yet with that steel-cold resolution
that few even of his strongest admirers have understood to be at the base, if not of his
genius, then certainly of his character, he plunged more and more – not into the
distraction of vice as so many of his contemporaries had done – but into an orgy of
work. He wrote and lectured ceaselessly. In 1892 he founded the Irish Literary
Society in Dublin. A new volume of his work, *The Countess Cathleen and Various*

Cover of an issue of
The Savoy, with an
illustration by
Aubrey Beardsley

Legends and Lyrics, appeared in the same year, and he wrote a play, *The Land of Heart's Desire*, which was produced in London in 1894. He had joined the Hermetic Order of the Golden Dawn in 1890; now, after Parnell's death, his theosophical studies with Madame Blavatsky, McGregor Mathers, and George Pollexfen were resumed with redoubled concentration, and verse reflecting these interests appeared in *The Yellow Book*. Then, after the trial of Oscar Wilde (who had had nothing to do with *The Yellow Book*, and whose only comment on it was that it was 'horrid, and not yellow at all'), and with the dismissal of Aubrey Beardsley from the post of art editor of *The Yellow Book*, the famous magazine now ceased to exist. Yeats, together with Beardsley, Symons and others, then brought out *The Savoy*,

'The Yellow
Book' and 'The
Savoy'

49

Arthur Symons

published by Leonard Smithers. Less successful but more distinguished than *The Yellow Book*, *The Savoy* only lasted for a few numbers. But in these numbers had appeared some of the best lyrics written by Yeats up to that time, and Beardsley's only prose work: some chapters of a delicately Rabelaisian novel called *Under the Hill*, a baroque fragment of genius illustrated with genius by the author.

Yeats still saw Maud Gonne frequently (in Dublin and in London and Paris), friendship being the mutely accepted bond between them. Yeats and she must both have known enough or heard enough, even in those reticent times, to understand that a profoundly intimate friendship untouched by romantic complications be- tween a heterosexual man and a heterosexual woman of approximately the same age is rarely possible. Indeed, their own relationship provided sufficient evidence of the difficulty, without any information on the subject from outside sources. But they wrestled with the problem, she with a sort of easy impatience with his 'foolishness', he with painful effort. The image in his heart of the turbulent goddess was kept in his heart: he ceased for a while to plead with her, and celebrated her beauty and his loneliness only in his verse. There she still appeared in his images of 'these red lips with all their mournful pride', of her who 'trod so sweetly proud as 'twere upon a cloud'.

One of the illustrations by Aubrey
Beardsley for his unfinished novel *Under the
Hill*

Aubrey Beardsley, by W. R. Sickert

Olivia Shakespear.
Yeats first met her
during the 1890s, and she
became a lifelong friend

In *The Picture of Dorian Gray* Wilde had written about the unscrupulousness of poets who could make a 'broken heart run into several editions'. It almost seems as if he was foreseeing the countless poems to Maud Gonne, all of them informed by the pain that Yeats was enduring in the cause of

> *that monstrous thing*
> *Returned and yet unrequited love.*

'The Wind among the Reeds' For Wilde's novel was published eight years before the appearance of Yeats' third volume of verse, *The Wind among the Reeds* (1899). For a long while it was widely believed that all the love-poems in this book, and in the books which followed it, were addressed to Maud Gonne. Yet there are some poems which point to another woman, perhaps to more than one. The lines

> *Until the axle break*
> *That keeps the stars in their round,*
> *And hands hurl in the deep*
> *The banners of East and West,*
> *And the girdle of light is unbound,*
> *Your breast will not lie by the breast*
> *Of your beloved in sleep*

Maud Gonne in 1897

For she had fiery blood
When I was young,
And trod so sweetly proud
As 'twere upon a cloud,
A woman Homer sung
That life and letters seem
But an heroic dream.

clearly refer to Maud Gonne. But when Yeats bids the curlew

cry no more in the air,
Or only to the water in the West;
Because your crying brings to my mind
Passion-dimmed eyes and long heavy hair
That was shaken out over my breast:
There is enough evil in the crying of wind

it seems plain that he is thinking of a different woman. The hair of Maud Gonne, if we believe the accepted story – and there is little reason to disbelieve it – had never been shaken out over the poet's breast, and if her eyes were 'passion-dimmed' it was her passion for Irish freedom that dimmed them, or possibly the passion which she felt for John MacBride, the revolutionary soldier, as active and as violent as herself, whom she ultimately married.

No, it was another to whom such lines were addressed, and the other was a beautiful dark woman to whom Yeats refers, in his unpublished autobiography, by the name 'Diana Vernon'. Yet in spite of her marriage to another, there is no doubt that where Maud Gonne had said 'No', 'Diana Vernon' said 'Yes', and for a while Yeats found peace in her devotion. Perhaps it was on her account that he left those rooms in the Temple which for some months (having left Bedford Park) he had shared with the poet and critic Arthur Symons, his closest London friend, and, in 1895, took the rooms in Woburn Buildings that were to be his London home until 1919.

The love affair with 'Diana Vernon' did not endure for long. In one of the poems in *The Wind among the Reeds* Yeats writes, in words which were quite plainly meant to reach the ears of the turbulent Maud Gonne:

> *I had a beautiful friend*
> *And dreamed that the old despair*
> *Would end in love in the end:*
> *She looked in my heart one day*
> *And saw your image was there;*
> *She has gone weeping away.*

But his relationship with 'Diana Vernon' had given the poet peace and repose. Indeed, the contrast between this tranquillity and his anguished passion for Maud Gonne is summarized in a lyric called 'Friends'. At the start of this poem Yeats describes his feeling for 'Diana Vernon', which passed undisturbed between 'mind and delighted mind'. Of Maud Gonne, he cries with a bitterness new to him that she

> *took*
> *All till my youth was gone.*

The poem poignantly contrasts these two loves in their essentials:

> *women that have wrought*
> *What joy is in my days:*
> *One because no thought,*
> *Nor those unpassing cares,*
> *No, not in these fifteen*
> *Many-times-troubled years,*
> *Could ever come between*
> *Mind and delighted mind . . .*
> *And what of her that took*
> *All till my youth was gone*
> *With scarce a pitying look?*
> *How could I praise that one?*

Until he met Maud Gonne, Yeats' sisters had believed that he was in love with Florence Farr, the distinguished actress and speaker of verse. It was to her that he dedicated *The Land of Heart's Desire*. In this lovely but well-nigh unactable dramatic poem, the principal character is the Faery Child. Played in 1894 by Dorothy

Woburn Place (formerly Woburn Buildings), London. From 1895 until 1919 Yeats, when in London, occupied rooms in No. 5, the second house from the left

Poster (designed by Aubrey Beardsley) announcing the first performance of *The Land of Heart's Desire* at the Avenue Theatre, Northumberland Avenue, London, on 29 March 1894, and (*right*) Winifred Fraser (as Máire Bruin) and Dorothy Paget (as the Faery Child) in the first production

Paget, a niece of Florence Farr, the part requires a performer who can combine the qualities of an actress, a speaker of mystical poetry, and a prima ballerina with the personality of a child, a task even more formidable than that which confronts Juliet herself (although the role is neither as long as Juliet's, nor, indeed, as magnificent). But in such matters of consistency the audiences of the period were not as exacting as those of today. Florence Farr herself was later to appear as Aleel in Yeats' *Countess Cathleen*, and Aleel, however ethereally poetic his utterance may be, is no more a woman's part than is Hamlet. Yet nobody seems to have protested.

Florence Farr

In the poem 'All Soul's Night', composed in 1920 after Florence Farr's death, Yeats was to write, using the name she took on marriage:

> *On Florence Emery I call the next,*
> *Who finding the first wrinkles on a face*
> *Admired and beautiful,*
> *And knowing that the future would be vexed*
> *With 'minished beauty, multiplied commonplace,*
> *Preferred to teach a school*
> *Away from neighbour or friend,*
> *Among dark skins, and there*
> *Permit foul years to wear*
> *Hidden from eyesight to the unnoticed end.*

In these lines Yeats contemplates the actress's determination to go to Ceylon as a teacher once her beauty had faded.

Edward Martyn, by Sarah Purser

Tulira Castle, Gort, County ▶
Galway, the house of Edward
Martyn. It was here that Yeats, Lady
Gregory and Martyn first discussed
their plans for an Irish national
theatre

Edward Martyn

Shortly after he had moved to Woburn Buildings, Yeats travelled to Ireland with Arthur Symons, who was paying his first visit to the country. The two poets apparently did not linger long in Dublin, but went on to Sligo and Aran (places of which Symons has written his own grave and enchanting impressions). Yeats then took Symons to Tulira Castle in County Galway to pay a call on Edward Martyn, to whom he had previously been introduced in London by Symons' friend George Moore. Yeats remembered Martyn as a heavy, countrified man, and as he and Symons approached Martyn's Irish house down its avenue he murmured, 'We shall be waited on by a barefooted servant.' Symons was doubtless thrilled at this prophecy, which, however, since the year was 1896, was almost certainly not fulfilled. Martyn lived in Tulira Castle with his mother, with many pictures of doubtful taste, and with a church organ on which, a devout Catholic and a lover of music, he played Palestrina for his own and his friends' delight, though probably not for Yeats' delight, since the poet was tone-deaf and understood 'no music but that of words'. Nevertheless, to hear music by Palestrina in a lonely castle must have seemed an irresistibly romantic notion to Yeats, and no doubt he listened patiently.

Lady Gregory

A carpet should have been spread for Lady Gregory's entrance into the life of Yeats, a red, regal carpet, although she, with her gently fervent patriotism, would perhaps have chosen a green one. During the Yeats–Symons visit to Tulira, she called at the castle and invited Yeats and Symons to lunch at Coole Park. Lady Gregory was a woman of forty-five, plainly dressed, with beautiful, serious brown eyes that seemed to see everything and understand everything except hunting, shooting, fishing and George Moore. Born in Roxborough House in County Galway in 1852, her maiden name was Augusta Persse, and she came of a family

58

who had settled in Galway in the seventeenth century. According to legend, her seven brothers inherited the daring and physical prowess which had characterized her ancestors – a long line of soldiers, huntsmen, and political participants in the Irish Parliament. In 1879 she married Sir William Gregory, a Galway landowner whose estates were at Coole Park. During the seventies and eighties she travelled with him on visits to Ceylon, India, England and Italy. In 1889 Sir William died – and his widow never remarried. She began to edit her late husband's autobiography and family papers; but her literary ambitions were to require a form of expression both more creative, and more closely involved with Irish national aspirations.

It is impossible to over-estimate her influence on Yeats. She was his friend and counsellor, an understanding eye in the tumultuous and haunted places of his mind. She was to help him more than he had ever been helped in his life, chiefly, and most significantly, by offering him access to her house at Coole. This became

'Lake at Coole', by Jack B. Yeats
The trees are in their autumn beauty,
The woodland paths are dry,
Under the October twilight the water
Mirrors a still sky.

Lady Augusta Gregory with Yeats at Coole Park.
'I doubt if I should have done much with my life but for her firmness and her care'.

The tree in Coole Park on which visitors carved their initials. Those of Yeats and Sean O'Casey can be seen in this photograph

Sir William and Lady Gregory in front of the house, Coole Park, in 1888. 'This house has enriched my soul out of measure because here life moves within restraint through gracious forms.'

Yeats' most important home; for more than thirty years he spent all his summers there, and often his winters. In the symmetry of that leisured, orderly house, among the woods and waters of Coole, he found a haven of peace which he never ceased to celebrate, nor ever reconciled himself to losing.

Though no one present may have been aware of it, the meeting in 1896 at Tulira Castle of Yeats (the author of *The Countess Cathleen*) and Lady Gregory (the future author of *The Rising of the Moon*) in the home of Edward Martyn (who was also writing a play, *The Heather Field*) was a historic occasion. For on that day the first seeds of the Irish Literary Theatre were sown. Yet nothing was settled at this first meeting at Tulira. It was in July of the following year, in the garden of the Irish home of Edward Martyn's friend Comte Florimond de Basterot (at Duras on the borders of Clare and Galway), that Yeats for the first time talked to Augusta Gregory about his long-cherished dream of creating a theatre for Irish plays, saying how he and Florence Farr had thought that perhaps some little hall in London would suit their purposes.

Although no one has recorded the fact, we may be certain that at this moment the brown eyes of Lady Gregory snapped. She disapproved of the idea of London being the birthplace of the new Irish drama. She was a rapid thinker, and could make sudden and often brilliant decisions in the manner of a great general (as has been mentioned, some of her ancestors were military men), and on the spot she offered both to give and to collect money to pay for the first performances in Dublin of plays by Yeats and Martyn. George Moore, who was just embarking on his mild oats affair with the Irish literary movement, was intrigued and enthusiastic, and became a collaborator in the venture. Martyn (whose play *The Heather Field* was now ready) was, for the moment, wildly excited.

And so, in spite of a number of those troubles inseparable from theatrical enterprise in any country; in spite of Martyn's apparently repeated resignations, which assumed the *mouvement perpetuel* of a musical form; in spite of George Moore's pardonably sceptical views on the proceedings; above all, perhaps, in spite of the self-contradictory quaintness of the title 'Literary Theatre', the project was finally realized. A society, named the Irish Literary Theatre, was formed, with Yeats, Martyn and Moore as its directors. It was announced in Ireland that, for three years in succession, performances of 'Irish and Celtic' plays would be given by the society in Dublin in the spring. Rehearsals were now begun in London for the first productions of *The Countess Cathleen* and *The Heather Field*; the first performances were scheduled to take place during the week following 8 May 1899 in the Antient Concert Rooms, Molesworth Street, Dublin. The title part of *The Countess Cathleen* was at first given to Florence Farr's young niece, Dorothy Paget, who had played the Faery Child in *The Land of Heart's Desire* in 1894 and who possessed a beautiful voice, but inevitably lacked experience. But George Moore, who had

The beginnings of the Irish Literary Theatre

George Moore, by Sir
William Rothenstein

decided to attend the rehearsals, insisted that the part should be given to Miss (later Dame) May Whitty.

'Moore has put a Miss Whitty to act Countess Cathleen,' Yeats wrote. 'She acts admirably, and has no sense of Rhythm whatever. . . . She enrages me at every moment, but she will make the part a success.' It may have enraged Maud Gonne, too, that a part which was obviously modelled on her own personality, in a play which Yeats had dedicated to herself, should be taken by an English actress. But she held her peace.

Shortly before *The Countess Cathleen* was due to be performed in Dublin, the production was suddenly threatened by a rumour which arose in the city that the play was theologically unorthodox. Martyn, terrified, consulted a monk, who denounced the text as heretical. Moore, enraged that Yeats' work should have been submitted for approval to a cleric, wrote a letter to Martyn which enraged Martyn so much that he in turn sent a letter to Yeats, announcing his resignation from the society. On the morning that Yeats received his letter, Martyn, in a highly agitated condition, visited the poet and Florence Farr, who were breakfasting at the Nassau Hotel, to confirm his resignation, which Yeats succeeded in persuading him to withdraw. An enemy of Yeats now published a pamphlet in which the poet and his play were attacked once more, whereupon Cardinal Logue (who had read the pamphlet but not the play) wrote a letter, published in a newspaper, to the effect that if *The Countess Cathleen* were indeed as represented in the pamphlet, then no

Arthur Griffith

Catholic should see it. Many Catholic friends of Yeats and his colleagues now withdrew their support, and a manifesto, deploring *The Countess Cathleen*, was signed by students at University College, one abstention being that of James Joyce. Arthur Griffith (later to be the first President of the Irish Free State) offered to bring demonstrators, who would 'applaud anything the Church did not like', from the docks to the theatre. Yeats, however, unwilling that the performances of his play should become anti-Catholic demonstrations, arranged for the Royal Irish Constabulary (the British police force which was then patrolling Ireland) to be present in order to guard them against interruption from students in the gallery: an action which displeased his nationalist admirers.

The first productions of the Irish Literary Theatre Despite these difficulties and hazards, *The Countess Cathleen* was, in the end, duly presented at the Antient Concert Rooms. All Dublin seemed to be up in arms, and each performance recalled the riot at the end of the second act of *Die Meistersinger von Nürnberg*, everyone in the audience shouting protests or counter-protests. Yeats emerged as both the hero and the villain of the hour. Above all (together with Lady Gregory, Martyn and Moore), he emerged as one of the founders of the new Irish theatre company which, after it had been given a new permanent home, was later to become known to the world as the Abbey.

The performances of Martyn's *The Heather Field* were not disturbed by controversy, and the play won approval both from the Dublin public and from two visiting English critics, one of whom was Sir Max Beerbohm. During its second season in 1900 the Irish Literary Theatre presented another play by Martyn (*Maeve*), and also *The Bending of the Bough*, a rewritten version, by George Moore, of Martyn's play

'Mr W. B. Yeats, presenting Mr George Moore to the Queen of the Fairies.' This cartoon by Sir Max Beerbohm satirizes Moore's initiation into the Irish literary movement, with which he was to carry on a brief and uneasy collaboration

The Tale of a Town. Then Yeats and Moore together wrote a play, based on an ancient legend, entitled *Diarmuid and Grania.* Their partnership, after the manner of an unsuitable marriage, went through various stages of storm, stress, sulks and strained silences. It also experimented, again in conjugal fashion, with many methods of readjustment. These involved Moore writing a script in French, this being then translated into Irish by Torna, a Gaelic poet, re-translated into Kiltartanese, a County Galway dialect of English, by Lady Gregory, and at last having 'style put on it' by Yeats. Naturally, this sequence of events led to the beginning

Miss A. E. Horniman

A scene from the first production of *Cathleen ni Houlihan* in Dublin in 1902. The title part was acted by Maud Gonne (in the picture on the left, standing on the right)

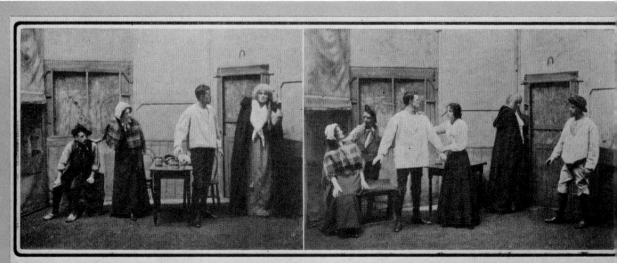

Many songs have been made about me. I heard one in the wind this morning   It is not a man going to his marriage that I look to for help

KORAN

LADY GREGORY
SIGHING FOR NEW WORLDS TO KILTARTANISE.

GRACE PLUNKETT

Lady Gregory, a cartoon by Grace Plunkett

of the end of any genuine friendship between Yeats and Moore; but the play, in what precise form it is now difficult to discover, was produced in October 1900 at the Gaiety Theatre, Dublin, with Frank Benson and his wife in the leading roles. This third season of the Irish Literary Theatre was the last with which Edward Martyn was associated; disagreeing with Yeats' determination that the society should concentrate on presenting plays of peasant life, he resigned. Finally.

These early productions of the new dramatic movement had necessarily been performed by English casts, since the society lacked the means of training Irish actors. But with the discovery by Yeats of the brothers Frank and William Fay, two genuine men of the theatre, this situation changed. The Fays, who happened to be Irish, were able to train a company of Irish amateur players. Successful performances of Yeats' new play were given (this was *Cathleen ni Houlihan*, written in one act, and on a patriotic theme) in St Teresa's Hall in 1902, with Maud Gonne in the title part. After the performances, the Irish Literary Theatre was replaced by a newly formed body, the Irish National Theatre, of which initially Yeats was President, and AE (George Russell), Douglas Hyde and Maud Gonne were Vice-presidents. Lady Gregory supported the venture, and so did Pádraic Colum and other young poets. The next year, the company received help from a new and powerful source. Miss A. E. Horniman, the English theatre manager and patron, who was playing such a vital part in organizing the modern repertory movement,

Miss A. E. Horniman

67

A design by Charles Ricketts for one of the
costumes in *The King's Threshold*

The old Abbey Theatre, Dublin

Sir Hugh Lane (*left*) and the directors of the Irish
National Theatre: J. M. Synge, Yeats (*foreground*)
and Lady Gregory. A drawing (1907) by Sir
William Orpen

was a friend and former secretary of Yeats. An admirer of his work, and of the
Irish dramatic movement, she now came to its assistance: first, by staging a new
play by Yeats (*The King's Threshold*), then by offering to provide and equip a new
theatre for the company, a promise which was fulfilled when, in 1904, the Abbey
Theatre was adapted from two existing buildings in Abbey Street, Dublin. It   *The Abbey*
opened in December, with productions of two plays: Yeats' *On Baile's Strand* and   *Theatre*
Lady Gregory's comedy *Spreading the News*.

Miss Horniman did not remain in Dublin (though she continued to be associated with the Irish National Theatre until 1910), and the Irish National Theatre
was now turned into a limited company, with Yeats, Lady Gregory and J. M. Synge,
whom Yeats had met eight years earlier, as directors. In the years that followed,
Yeats watched the slow development of the Abbey Theatre, working with Lady
Gregory at the making of plays, at the reading of plays by other authors which were
submitted to them, sometimes at the pulling together of promising works, sometimes at the dismal task of rejection. There were also battles to be fought with Dublin
Castle on the matter of the theatre patents.

The cover of an Abbey Theatre programme

The Fay brothers, who led the theatre company, attracted to it some remarkable talents. Outstanding among these were the sisters Sara Allgood and Máire O'Neill, and there was also Máire Nic Shiubhlaigh, who had a fine dramatic instinct and a voice almost as wonderful as that of Allgood herself. Among the men were Joseph Kerrigan, Arthur Sinclair, Dudley Digges, Fred O'Donovan, J. J. O'Rourke, and Sydney Morgan. All these members of the original Irish National Theatre company were actors by right of birth: what they lacked was experience. Perhaps, for a paradoxical reason, this was to prove fortunate. Sarah Allgood has often told the true story of how these actors developed one of their most admired qualities: their stillness; their strange repose on the stage; their economy of gesture and movement which aroused so much astonishment in English and American critics, weary of the complicated style of acting then fashionable in London and New York. 'It was Willie Fay's brilliance really', she explained, 'he didn't let us move a muscle or stir a foot unless it was desperately necessary: he knew damn well we weren't able to do it.' And so the cast remained motionless, 'mystic, wonderful': the women wrapped in their shawls, the men in their rough clothes, their heavy boots seemingly rooted to the ground; on their mobile lips the words of Yeats, Lady Gregory, Pádraic Colum, and later of John Millington Synge himself. And Broadway and the West End went wild with enthusiasm.

70

William Fay, by John Butler Yeats

Actors of the Abbey Theatre Company performing *Cathleen ni Houlihan*. From left to right: Máire O'Neill, Frank Fay, Sara Allgood and Joseph Kerrigan. The economy of gesture for which the company was so much admired is well shown in this drawing by Ben Bay

KATHLEEN-NI-HOULIHAN.

BRIDGET GILLANE,
MISS MARIE O'NEILL.

PETER GILLANE,
MR FRANK J. FAY.

KATHLEEN-NI-HOULIHAN,
MISS SARA ALLGOOD.

MICHAEL GILLANE,
MR J. M. KERRIGAN

Two poets whom Yeats met in Paris:
Stéphane Mallarmé and (*right*) Paul
Verlaine

J. M. Synge Synge was the greatest playwright whom the Irish dramatic movement produced, and his meeting with Yeats in Paris in 1896 proved to be one of the most important events in the history of the Irish literary revival. Like other English-speaking writers of the period, Yeats had every now and then visited Paris during the 1890s, staying sometimes with McGregor Mathers and his wife who were living there. Yeats' French was the usual French of the English speaker, scanty and inadequate. But he met Mallarmé (with whose work his own had much in common), Villiers de l'Isle-Adam (whom he admired and frequently quoted) and Paul Verlaine (who spoke enough English to amuse him with his comments on Tennyson). More significantly, while he was staying in a small hotel in the Place de l'Odéon during 1896, he met there a fellow guest, an unknown young man named John Millington Synge, who had lived for a while in Aran and knew enough of the Irish language to talk with the island people. Yeats met Synge in the course of later visits to Paris, and during one of these, in a moment of uncanny insight (for how could he have guessed at the qualities hidden away in the mind of this uncommunicative

72

young man?) he persuaded him to return to Ireland. 'Go back to Aran. . . . You will write our satirical masterpiece,' he announced, and when Synge told him that if he were to live in such wild Atlantic places as the Aran Islands for any length of time he would soon be dead, Yeats said impressively, 'Not before you have written your masterpiece!'

This reply was characteristic of Yeats, who was indifferent to all things in the lives of others but their purpose in the world of art and in serving the destiny of Ireland; and, as so often happened, he was proved to be right. Synge obeyed him and returned to Ireland.

All the best work that Synge created during his short life, overshadowed as it was by illness, was written for the Irish stage. His masterpiece, *The Playboy of the Western World*, completed while he was still in good health, was produced at the Abbey Theatre in 1907. In this tragic comedy he revealed the country people of western Ireland with a penetrating, relentless insight which was widely mistaken by the Irish for ridicule. The performances of the play at the Abbey Theatre, and

J. M. Synge, a photograph taken on 31
December 1895

John Synge, I and Augusta Gregory thought
All that we did, all that we said or sang
Must come from contact with the soil, from that
Contact everything Antaeus-like grew strong.

The Aran Islands, County Galway, in the
1890s

Sara Allgood, Barry Fitzgerald
(*centre*) and Arthur Shields in a scene
from a production of Synge's *The
Playboy of the Western World* at the
Abbey Theatre

several years later in America, caused riots of protest, and for a while Synge, not
Yeats, was the villainous hero of the Irish hour. He did not quite finish revising his
last play – the powerful, piteous *Déirdre of the Sorrows* – before his death in a Dublin
nursing home on 24 March 1909.

Synge was the first and last dramatist who combined the quality of the Yeatsian
hope for a poetic theatre with the grim, earthy and violent sense of comedy that
outraged the fools and turned the heads of the wise men, and, incidentally, filled
the theatre for the first time. Synge, also, with his ear for Gaelic and for that transi-
tory form of English moulded by Gaelic echoes that was still spoken by the
country people in places where the newer tongue was slowly replacing the older (for
what is the language of Synge and Lady Gregory but the accidental beauty of
broken English?), Synge was the man who prepared the way for Seán O'Casey
and for the less spectacular interpreters of Irish life who preceded and followed him.
Synge, in fact, was the man for whose coming Yeats had prayed, the man whose
disciples, in the way of disciples, imitated his mannerisms, lacked his genius and
broke the image of the older poet's dream for a theatre whose plays he had declared
should be 'for the most part remote, spiritual and ideal'. As it was, the Abbey
Theatre became a paradise for the realist, and Yeats, in a letter to Lady Gregory,
was to describe its growing success with the public as 'a discouragement and a
defeat'.

He had not wanted that sort of theatre; it did not really want him. To this day, its
most accomplished actors and directors have been at their best in the interpretation

Two cartoons: Yeats addressing the audience from the stage of the Abbey Theatre and (*below*) Sir Hugh Lane keeping the peace during a performance of *The Playboy of the Western World*

Yeats, a caricature (1915) by Edmund Dulac. Still cherishing his dream of establishing a poetic national theatre in Ireland, Yeats viewed with disfavour the trend towards realism which Synge's plays had launched at the Abbey Theatre. His continued collaboration with the company, with whose aims he was no longer in sympathy, is here satirized by Dulac

Yeats' disappointment with the Irish theatre of almost any Irish dramatist whose name one can remember sooner than that of its original prophet. It was almost certainly this disappointment with the popular theatre (and the theatre, at its best and worst, is essentially a popular art, as the Greeks knew, as Shakespeare knew) that led Yeats at last to seek a new approach to the writing of plays. For he still wanted to write them: he still believed himself to be a dramatist; he still longed for an audience, for listeners to the spoken word rather than for readers of the printed page. So it came to pass that years later he was to turn for his hearers to the cultivated drawing room, for his manner and method to the Japanese *Noh* play, because he wished to evoke emotions that should have as little as possible to do with the formula of the European public stage. His *Plays for Dancers* were written for dancers who would be not only silent but masked; for

Lennox Robinson

players in whom the art of acting would be replaced by the arts of mime and the chanting of verse; for musicians who would be skilled in the use of flute and drum and gong.

In 1910, the year after Synge's death, the Abbey Theatre lost the help of another of its strongest supporters: Miss Horniman. When King Edward VII died on 7 May, Miss Horniman's loyalty to England (which, whether she approved of its government of Ireland or not, was still her own country) told her in no uncertain voice that the Abbey Theatre should close its doors that day, and she apparently assumed that this action would be taken. The young and highly talented Lennox Robinson (who had succeeded Yeats as manager of the theatre) thought differently, and became involved in a comedy of errors in which he, Lady Gregory and a Rustic Messenger played the leading roles. Perplexed by the news that all the other Dublin theatres were closing on account of the royal demise, Robinson sent a telegram to Coole Park asking for advice. Lady Gregory wired back, 'Should close through courtesy.' But since the messenger boy, presumably an adept in the art of walking as slowly as possible, had taken three hours to reach Lady Gregory's house at Coole and return to his post office at Gort (a total distance of four miles), the matinée at the Abbey Theatre was in full swing by the time the Gregorian advice was delivered, and it was considered too late, at that stage, to cancel the evening performance.

Yeats was in France at the time, and knew nothing of these events. On his return to Woburn Buildings, he was astonished to learn of what had passed, and that

4 The scene is Coole

The woods are in their autumn colours
But the lake waters are low
[...] the footfalls she
The path way has [...] to [...]
And [...] the [...] half light?
In the half dark & [...]
indolently away, the shadow & the grey shore
[...]

As number the swans, as number the swans
[...] in shadows, grey shore & number the swans
indolently away the shore

Floating, among the shore.

We are now at the nineteenth autumn
Since I first made my count.
I [...] to soar to by the heard me
[...] the loud wings

[...]
as wheel above the water in great broken rings
and a slow clamour of wings.

But now they drift on the still water
Mysterious, beautiful
among what rushes are they [...]
where by the [...]

Miss Horniman withdraws her subsidy from the Abbey Theatre

Miss Horniman had threatened to withdraw her subsidy from the Abbey Theatre unless 'an apology from the Directors and Robinson' was published in the Dublin press. Lady Gregory duly published an apology, which Miss Horniman rejected as inadequate. Yeats would not issue any further apology, and finally Miss Horniman withdrew her subsidy on the grounds that the directors, by allowing the theatre to remain open on the day of the King's death, had contravened one of the conditions upon which the subsidy had been granted: namely, that the theatre should not be used for political purposes. But the Abbey Theatre (which had already survived the riots which attended the first production of *The Playboy of the Western World*)

(*Opposite and right*) Parts of two drafts by Yeats for 'The Wild Swans at Coole', the first poem in the volume, bearing the same title, which was published in 1919

was now well enough established to continue without Miss Horniman's help.

Throughout this time Yeats found his most frequent refuge from the brawl and tumult of the stage in the peace of the countryside. He would fly from the tedium of board meetings and actors' disputes and city traffic – a constant menace to his safety, for he was an erratic pedestrian – and back he would go to the West, to the wilderness of birds and leaves and shadows where he could continue with his true business of writing poetry. Once again it was Lady Gregory who, with her house at Coole Park, provided the setting for the work which Yeats created during the first dozen or so years of this century.

One of the rooms occupied by Yeats in Woburn Buildings from 1895 until 1919

They were eventful years. In 1903 a group of essays on the arts, on Spenser and Shelley and Blake, on Ireland and on Magic were published under the title *Ideas of Good and Evil*, as well as a long narrative poem, *Baile and Aillin*, and a new book of verse, *In the Seven Woods*. In 1905 Yeats' most elaborate dramatic poem for the theatre, *The Shadowy Waters* (written some years earlier at Coole), was produced in London; Yeats then rewrote it, and the revised version was published in 1906. In 1907 the poet visited Italy; this was the first occasion on which his footfall 'lit in the green shadow of Ferrara wall'. A year later his *Collected Works in Verse and Prose* was published, and in 1910 he was granted a Civil List pension and found himself on the Academic Committee of the Royal Society of Literature. His visits to Dublin at this time were spent in an hotel; in London he kept to his rooms in Woburn Buildings, where his writing-table, armchair and 'great blue curtain' were Lady Gregory's gifts. But his most creative weeks and months

82

The library, Coole Park. A sketch by Yeats, who, writes Lady Gregory, took 'delight in the mere appearance of these walls of leather and vellum, mellowed by passing centuries, in the sudden illumination of golden ornament and lettering as the sun sails towards the western hills'

were passed in County Galway. Sligo had receded from the foreground of his thoughts for the time being; and now it was the woods and waters about Lady Gregory's house at Coole that were celebrated in so many of his songs.

Towards the end of this prolific period Yeats' style underwent a profound change. *Change in style* The romantic wistfulness, the dreamy, decorative quality of much of his earlier *of Yeats' poetry* verse now gave way to a manner at once more terse, astringent and masculine, which became apparent in a new volume, *The Green Helmet and other Poems*, published in 1910, and even more strikingly evident in the next volume of poems, *Responsibilities* (1914). 'The Fascination of What's Difficult' (quoted on page 38) and 'The Grey Rock' (quoted on page 45) are examples of this new style, which Yeats probably felt, with justification, to be better suited than his earlier manner to the increasingly varied and public nature of his themes. But this remarkable new phase also drew from him some of his most magnificent love poems, such as the one that

83

begins 'She lived in storm and strife' (quoted on page 46) from *Responsibilities*.

In one of the poems in this book, 'September 1913', Yeats looked about him at the country which he had served with such devotion and found nothing but disillusion. Seeing with sudden bitter clarity the littleness, the greyness, the meanness, the self-glorification, the prudish savagery and false piety gathering – as it seemed, incurably – over the face of the land and her people, he cried:

> *Romantic Ireland's dead and gone,*
> *It's with O'Leary in the grave.*

The Easter Rising, 1916
It would seem to the single-minded imagination, unhampered by any legion of detailed facts, that the rising of the Irish Republican volunteers in Easter Week, 1916, was a direct answer to the melancholy challenge of Yeats' September poem. It is strange that his nostrils, usually sensitive to the approach of a storm as the nostrils of cat or horse, or of some nervous woman, seemed unaware of the gathering of the hosts of battle. But it was so: he sensed nothing at all. Nevertheless, the Easter Week Rising – from any point of view the most considerable of all Irish demonstrations of the ancient feud – certainly did take place, and when he heard of it the poet was deeply moved. His poem 'Easter 1916', composed within a few weeks of the executions of the leaders of the rising, remains one of his finest. Its recurring couplet, with its insistent, irregular, beaten-out rhythm, like that of mournful bells, has become to Irish ears as familiar as a nightly prayer:

> *All changed, changed utterly :*
> *A terrible beauty is born.*

The Countess Markievicz
In another poem, 'On a Political Prisoner', Yeats thinks of a woman who had helped to lead the rebellion and who had been a constant image among his early memories. This was not Maud Gonne but the Countess Markievicz, who, before her marriage, had been Constance Gore-Booth of Lissadell in the County Sligo. Dreaming of her, as she lay in prison under sentence of death – this was later lifted – throughout the spring and summer of 1916, Yeats writes of her giving bread to a seagull through the bars of the windows of her cell. And he wonders whether, touching 'that lone wing', she remembers her childhood in her own western countryside where, as a boy, he had often watched her riding 'under Ben Bulben to the meet', the loveliest young woman of the county, herself as young and free as the seagull which she was now feeding with crumbs through the bars of her prison window.

From the time of the Easter Rising of 1916 up to the Civil War of 1922, Yeats was more affected by public events than he had been since 1898 when, under the influence of Maud Gonne, he had joined the Commemoration Committee of the Insurrection of 1798. Perhaps he was even more deeply affected than he had been

84

The Countess Markievicz (*left*) and a friend on horseback

When long ago I saw her ride
Under Ben Bulben to the meet,
The beauty of her country-side
With all youth's lonely wildness stirred,
She seemed to have grown clean and sweet
Like any rock-bred, sea-borne bird.

(*Above*) The Countess Markievicz in the cellar of Liberty Hall, Dublin, Easter 1916. It was in Liberty Hall that the Irish Nationalist leaders planned the rising and issued their orders

(*Right*) Liberty Hall, after it had been bombarded by a British gunboat on the River Liffey

Lissadell House, County Sligo, the home of the Gore-Booth family

The light of evening, Lissadell,
Great windows open to the south.

O'Connell Street, Dublin, showing the ruins of the burnt-out General Post Office, which had been the headquarters of the Irish Nationalists during the Easter Rising of 1916

The statue of Cú Chulainn, General Post Office, Dublin, erected as a memorial to the executed leaders of the Easter Rising

Major John MacBride

then. For now no personal amorous emotion was involved, nor was it the faded romance of a hundred years ago that set his heart abeat, but the violent romance, the reality and the terror of the present. Although it is likely that he fought against the intrusion of public affairs upon his mind, it was difficult for him to ignore them altogether: any aspect of Ireland's destiny was too close, the pressures of the time too insistent, for him to remain indifferent, even to remain silent. Much of the poetry of this period (in the volumes *The Wild Swans at Coole* and *Michael Robartes and the Dancer*) reflects the clash of current events. It was as though a new imagination had not banished the old but had invaded its ancient dwelling-place and created a new order: Caoilte and Niamh of the Sidhe, the Host of Faery, were now called by the names of the executed soldiers of Easter Week. Pádraic Pearse, the most famous of the leaders, standing among his men in the burning Post Office, the headquarters for seven days of the Irish Republican Army, Yeats wrote, had 'summoned Cú Chulainn to his side'.

Politics and Yeats' poetry

One of the men who had been executed in 1916 for taking part in the Easter Rising was Major John MacBride, whom Maud Gonne had married in 1903 and from whom she was separated a few years later. In 1917 Yeats for the last time proposed to Maud Gonne, and for the last time she refused him. A few months later he proposed to her adopted daughter, the almost equally beautiful Iseult Gonne,

Iseult Stuart (*née* Gonne), by
AE (George Russell)

Maud MacBride (*née* Gonne; seated, with hat
on lap) visiting women on hunger strike in
Mountjoy Prison, Dublin

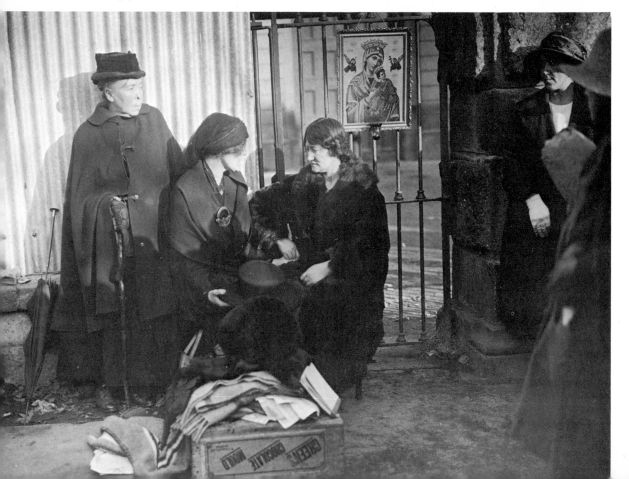

George Hyde-Lees,
whom Yeats married
in 1917

and she also refused him. But marriage must have been in his stars as well as in his thoughts at that time, for a little later in the same year he proposed to George Hyde-Lees, an English lady of great charm and culture, and she accepted him. The two had been introduced in 1911 by Yeats' friend Olivia Shakespear and by her brother, Mr Tucker, and his wife, who was the mother (by her first marriage) of Yeats' future wife. Although little has been recounted of this first meeting (which took place at the Tuckers' country house in Devonshire) it is likely that the young lady carried the image of the Irish poet in her mind during the years that followed.

George Hyde-Lees must have been of an adventurous and liberal tempera- *Marriage* ment, for the country to which her husband was to bring her was in the throes of its last struggle for independence, and emotions were at a high pitch. And, indeed, although the animosity felt in Ireland against English government at that time was seldom, if ever, directed against English individuals, many English people felt that it must surely be so directed, and many Englishwomen would have hesitated at the prospect of visiting a nation at grips with their own nation, let alone of joining it, so to speak, in wedlock. But that is what George Hyde-Lees did after her marriage to Yeats in a London registry office on 21 October 1917, and matters turned out very happily. Mrs Yeats was loved and accepted by the Irish people from the begin- ning, and seems from the beginning to have loved and understood them.

Her husband did not, however, force an Irish residence on her immediately. The couple settled for a while, not in Yeats' country, but in his wife's, where they

A sketch by John Butler Yeats in a letter to Yeats dated 13 April 1918. It shows Yeats and his wife (whom Yeats' father had not yet met) fishing in a river in Galway

lived first in Yeats' rooms in Woburn Buildings, then at Oxford, where they took a house in Broad Street in January 1918. Early that year Yeats published a volume of essays on mystical subjects, *Per Amica Silentia Lunae*, which showed that his passionate interest in the hidden world had not diminished. Indeed, marital content seems to have increased it, especially since his wife (who had begun to attempt automatic writing on their honeymoon) soon developed the gift of mediumship, with the result that thereafter the couple together carried out many experiments in occult practice.

Thoor Ballylee   Later in 1918 the Yeatses travelled to Ireland, where they lived at first in Dublin. Several years previously Yeats had bought a Norman tower, with two cottages attached to it, at the village of Ballylee in Galway, and the couple now set about restoring this property with a view to making it their summer residence. Ballylee (where Mary Hynes, the beloved of the Gaelic poet Raftery, had lived in the early years of the nineteenth century) is about a morning's walk from Coole Park and four miles from the town of Gort. The name of the high, square tower, 'Túr Bail' i Liaigh', was given by Yeats the English-sounding form 'Thoor Ballylee'. Yeats' insistence on spelling Irish names according to English phonetics (an awkward practice, since no logical phonetic system exists in English) was the only English trait in his character. It is also of course an Irish trait: if a people do not respect the spelling of their own language how can they expect that their conquerors will? In 1919 the Yeatses moved into 'Thoor Ballylee', and Yeats dedicated the tower to his wife in a short and lovely poem which ends with the ominous prophetic couplet:

> *And may these characters remain*
> *When all is ruin once again.*

92

I the poet William Yeats.
With old millboards and
  sea-green slates.
And smithy work from
  the Gort forge.
Restored this tower
  for my wife George.
And may these characters
  remain
When all is ruin once again.

'Thoor Ballylee', Gort, County Galway,
the summer home of the Yeatses from 1919
until 1929

An ancient bridge, and a more ancient tower,
A farmhouse that is sheltered by its wall,
An acre of stony ground,
Where the symbolic rose can break in flower,
Old ragged elms, old thorns innumerable,
The sound of the rain or sound
Of every wind that blows;
The stilted water-hen
Crossing stream again
Scared by the splashing of a dozen cows.

Stone at 'Thoor Ballylee', inscribed with
the poem in which Yeats dedicated the
tower to his wife

93

Yeats with his two
children, Anne and
Michael

After Yeats' death all was indeed 'ruin once again', but today, owing to the work
of Mrs Mary Hanley of Limerick and other loyal devotees, the tower has, happily,
been restored once more, and today 'Thoor Ballylee' is much as it was in the poet's
lifetime.

On 24 February 1919, before the Yeatses moved into 'Thoor Ballylee', a
daughter, Anne, was born to them in Dublin. It was perhaps from her mother's
side that Anne inherited her steady intelligence, her tranquil, friendly charm;
from her father's the marked gift which she was to develop as a painter. In October
Yeats, together with his wife, travelled to the United States and conducted there a
highly successful lecture tour which lasted until May 1920 and in the course of
which he read and discussed his poetry. The Yeatses then returned to Oxford,
remaining there, or in the neighbourhood, until early 1922. In August 1921 their
daughter Anne had been joined by a brother, Michael, born at Thame, who grew

82 Merrion Square, Dublin, the house which the Yeatses took in 1922. AE (George Russell) was living at No. 84 while the Yeatses were in residence in the square

up to look very much as his father must have looked in the eighties and nineties, and who has become (as his father was shortly to become) a member of Seanad Éireann, the Irish Senate. Early in 1922 Yeats bought a house at 82 Merrion Square, Dublin, and in the spring he and his family moved there. They returned to an Ireland that was on the brink of the civil war precipitated by the establishment, on 6 December 1921, of the constitution of the Irish Free State.

During the 1920s, and the first few years of the following decade, Yeats was inevitably affected by the upheaval and change that were taking place not only in his own country, but also in the entire life of what is persistently called the civilized world. The 1914–18 war had turned all things upside down as completely as the war of 1939–45 was later to do, and in a manner which was far harder to anticipate. Social values were banished or inverted, social behaviour was altered, a passion for frankness and for individual freedom of speech and self-revelation, prompted

95

perhaps by the discovery outside central Europe of Freud and his theories of psychoanalysis, created a new society in which the terror of 'repression' became the order of the day. This trend went hand in fashionable hand with a reaction against romanticism and nationalism alike, and, if Yeats himself had not been such a vital and violent personality, he and all that he represented might have suffered something very like eclipse. As it was, the modern spirit was manifest everywhere as a more marked, more self-conscious and much more widely adopted mode of thinking than had existed since the *Zeitgeist* of the 1890s, when such preoccupations had been for the most part confined to the educated classes. The strenuous, self-assertive mood of the twenties even entered the Abbey Theatre, where Lennox Robinson, always a barometer of the changing times, had begun to write plays which reflected a life not necessarily Irish at all but vaguely international, and Yeats himself had already finished *The Player Queen*, the first and only play of his to be set not in Ireland but in some nameless, lunar no man's land.

The 1920s also saw the beginning and end of the Irish Civil War; the firm enthronement of James Joyce as Ireland's latest and most alarming interpreter; the discovery of new writers like Frank O'Connor, Seán ó Faoláin, Liam O'Flaherty and the dramatists Seán O'Casey and Denis Johnston; the creation by an Englishman (Hilton Edwards) and an Irishman (the present writer) of the Dublin Gate Theatre, with its introduction into Ireland of the methods of Expressionism and its international repertoire, and the establishment by the present writer in Galway of Taibhdhearc na Gaillimhe, the only Irish-speaking theatre in the world.

At the beginning of this period, in the early 1920s, Yeats and his wife found themselves in an Ireland which was at once rebellious, active, joyous, defiant, up in

The Gate Theatre, Dublin

Yeats at a garden party at the house of Oliver St John Gogarty in 1923. From left to right: front row, Yeats, Compton Mackenzie, Augustus John, Sir Edwin Lutyens; back row, G. K. Chesterton, James Stephens, Lennox Robinson

arms, inflamed with love and hate, and deeply orthodox in matters of religious observance. To most Irishmen at this time, the preoccupation with the occult of Yeats and his wife must have seemed uncanny, obscure, cranky and heretical. Nevertheless, whatever misgivings they may have felt in the matter, the unalterably conservative, profoundly cynical, inexplicably tolerant Irish, as represented by their grand new Free State Government, offered Yeats, in the turbulent year 1922, a seat in the Irish Senate, which the poet accepted and took up on 13 January 1923. *Takes seat in the Irish Senate*

And so he became, as later he described himself, the 'sixty-year-old smiling public man' – stiff collar, formal tie, striped trousers, top hat and all. In this garb he looked suitably and rather endearingly lost, as a poet and mystic should. Or

Yeats in 1923

perhaps it was the mystic in him that prevented him from being lost. The true mystic, like the perfect gentleman, is seldom lost: that may be the advantage of there being so many incarnations behind the one as there are so many ancestors behind the other. No, he was not lost: he made in fact an impressive and able figure in Irish public life, though one may be sure that the power of mediumship that had developed in his wife interested him far more than the meetings of the Senate.

The public events which were a part of Ireland's history, those violent, pragmatical forces that had knocked so insistently at the door of 'Thoor Ballylee' and at the door of Yeats' mind during the Civil War, left deep traces on him. Yet he seems invariably to have recoiled, at some moment or other, from the 'affable Irregular', with his jokes about guns and ambushes and sudden death, away from the 'brown Lieutenant and his men, Halfdressed in national uniform', back to his own inner life again, to

> turn towards my chamber, caught
> In the cold snows of a dream.

98

He would pace up and down at night on the battlemented roof of his tower; alone above domestic life, alone with the running stream, the sighing of the wind, the bare Galway hills below him and above him the cold stars. Did Owen Aherne and Michael Robartes, those ghostly second selves whom he had invoked long years before, walk invisible by his side? Did Red Hanrahan accompany him there? What phantoms haunted him now? What dreams of his own soul, what visions of blood-drenched battle-fields were clamouring in him now 'to beg the voice and utterance of their tongue'?

During 1923 Yeats was awarded the Nobel Prize for Literature, which was *Nobel Prize* presented to him by the King of Sweden, and two years later he published his appreciation in a short work, *The Bounty of Sweden*. In 1925 there also appeared

The award of the Nobel Prize to Yeats in 1923. The presentation ceremony in the Hall of the Swedish Academy, Stockholm, on 10 December. Yeats can be seen among the seated group on the dais, fourth from the left

Seán O'Casey

'A Vision' his most elaborate book in prose, a work in which he brings in Plato and Plotinus as well as certain modern philosophers to corroborate his own astrological, mystical and historical theories. These were founded partly on his long quest for some form of ultimate religious conviction, and partly on the communications which he and his wife had received 'from invisible forces'. The elements that compose the book are derived from what he describes as 'an incredible experience', and they are set forth with as much learned clarity as may be applied to the mysteries of the relationship of the soul to time and eternity. This was the most formidable declaration of the conclusions which he had spent his life in reaching: he called the book *A Vision*.

In 1926 he produced a translation of Sophocles' *Oedipus the King* which was presented at the Abbey Theatre in the same year. He defended Seán O'Casey when, at the first performance of *The Plough and the Stars*, the play was howled down by outraged sections of the audience. 'You have disgraced yourselves again,' he cried in majestic fury from the stage, remembering no doubt the similar howls that had arisen about the ears of Synge on the first night of *The Playboy of the Western World* so many years ago. In 1927 he made a translation of Sophocles' *Oedipus at Colonus* (which, like its predecessor, was produced in the same year at the Abbey Theatre), he also delivered resounding speeches in the Senate on coinage and copyright; then, severely weakened by attacks of lung congestion and influenza, *Moves to Rapallo to recover health* he was ordered abroad for a complete rest. Accordingly, early in 1928 Yeats, with his wife and their two children, moved to Rapallo.

In the same year he wrote and published a long essay on the death of Synge. (It appeared in a book entitled *The Death of Synge, and Other Passages from an Old*

Diary.) He also published a new volume of verse, *The Tower*. This set him indisputably among the greatest living poets of the English language. His genius is at its height in these 36 poems, with their superb imagery, their perfection of form, and their ominous hatred of age and death.

'This is an indescribably lovely place,' the poet wrote to Lady Gregory from Rapallo, 'like some little Greek town one imagines. . . . Here I shall put off the bitterness of Irish quarrels and write my most amiable verses. . . . Re-reading *The Tower*,' he continued, 'I was astonished at its bitterness.' But what he saw as mere bitterness was viewed by certain critics as an immortal fury against the tragedy of decay, the inevitability of death. And it is this emotion that evokes in his mind a bizarre, strangely assured speculation on life after death in one of the poems in the book: 'Sailing to Byzantium'. There he celebrates what man can create, and rejects the way in which man himself has been created, the ill-starred slave of his inevitable passing into dust:

> *Once out of nature I shall never take*
> *My bodily form from any natural thing,*
> *But such a form as Grecian goldsmiths make*
> *Of hammered gold and gold enamelling*
> *To keep a drowsy Emperor awake;*
> *Or set upon a golden bough to sing*
> *To lords and ladies of Byzantium*
> *Of what is past, or passing, or to come.*

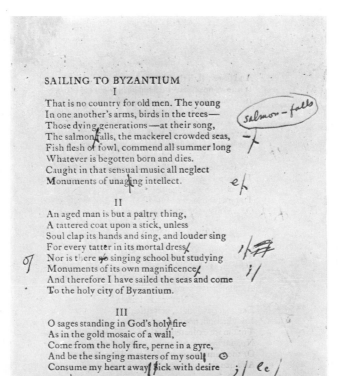

Part of a proof of
'Sailing to Byzantium',
with Yeats' corrections

Ezra Pound, who influenced Yeats by his creatively critical comments on the Irish poet's work. 'He is full of the middle ages and helps me to get back to the definite and the concrete away from modern abstractions. To talk a poem over with him is like getting you to put a sentence into dialect. All becomes clear and natural.'

Term of office in the Senate ends In April he returned to Ireland, and on 18 July gave his last speech to the Senate; his term of office was now over, and, on account of his poor health, he did not seek re-election. At the onset of winter he returned (again for reasons of health) to Rapallo, where he wrote the prose work, based on his psychic experiences, entitled *A Packet for Ezra Pound*. (The American poet had become a close friend.) As he told his friend Olivia Shakespear in a letter, he spent the rest of his time at Rapallo

'sitting in the sun when not reading or writing. I have written eleven lyrics in the past two months – nine of them "words for music", these last unlike my past work – wilder and perhaps slighter. Here is a lullaby that I like: a mother sings to her child

> *Beloved, may your sleep be sound*
> *That have found it where you fed.*
> *What were all the world's alarms*
> *To mighty Paris when he found*
> *Sleep upon a golden bed*
> *That first dawn in Helen's arms?*

TWO PLAYS FOR DANCERS
BY W. B. YEATS

MONCEROSDEASTRIS

THE CUALA PRESS
MCMXIX

The title-page of the first
edition of *Two Plays for
Dancers*, published in 1919
by the Cuala Press, Dublin.
The Cuala Press was
founded by Yeats' sisters,
Susan and Elizabeth

In the spring of 1929 the poet and his family went back to Ireland. That summer marked Yeats' last visit to 'Thoor Ballylee' and the production at the Abbey Theatre of *Fighting the Waves*, one of the *Plays for Dancers*, for which Ninette de Valois had created the choreography. The poet also visited Lady Gregory and started work on a long poem in celebration of Coole Park and of the generosity and grace that pervaded it. Back once more in Rapallo for the winter months, he was laid low with what was known as Maltese fever and for many weeks was kept to his bed. But, with the coming of spring, he had recovered sufficiently to tell Olivia Shakespear, in a letter dated 4 March 1930:

'I go out every day for an hour or two but have discovered that I must spend the rest of each day in my bed and there read nothing but story-books. Having exhausted the detective literature of the world I have just started upon the Wild West and shall probably, if my illness lasts long enough, descend to Buffalo Bill.'

But in April he was at work again. He now began to write a play in what, for him, was a strangely realistic manner, describing a séance held by a spiritualist medium (a woman), through whose lips the ghosts of Jonathan Swift, Stella and Vanessa speak. He gave it the title *The Words upon the Window Pane*. It was first performed at

the Abbey Theatre on 30 December 1930 under the direction of Lennox Robinson, and proved to be one of the most successful of Yeats' plays: a fact which seemed not only to please the poet but to astound him.

Because of Lady Gregory's advancing age and the painful illness that continually made her pass the night without sleep, Yeats stayed in Ireland throughout the winters of 1930 and 1931. In 1931 he was offered the honorary degree of Doctor of Letters by Oxford University, and he travelled to England to receive it. He spent the summer at Coole, and a sad summer it must have been, for Lady Gregory's *Death of Lady* health grew worse and worse. She lived on through the autumn and winter, but on *Gregory* 22 May 1932 she died. The next day Yeats wrote to Olivia Shakespear:

Lady Gregory in old age
I am in despair that time may bring
Approved patterns of women or of men
But not that selfsame excellence again.

The Avenue, Coole Park
I have heard the pigeons of the Seven Woods
Make their faint thunder, and the garden-bees
Hum in the lime-tree flowers.

'I had come to Dublin for a few days to see about Abbey business. On Sunday night at 11.30 I had a telephone message from her solicitor who had been trying to find me all day. I took the first train in the morning but she had died in the night. She was her indomitable self to the last but of that I will not write or not now.'

Many years before he had celebrated the importance in his life of this beloved woman. 'She has been to me mother, friend, sister and brother', he wrote in his diary in 1909, when she was ill. 'I cannot realize the world without her. She brought to my wandering thoughts steadfast nobility. All day the thought of losing her is like a conflagration among the rafters. Friendship is all the house I have.'

105

And now, in 1932, Lady Gregory was dead, and life, for Yeats, was never to be quite the same again.

Though he himself was once more in poor health during 1932, in October he undertook a lecture tour in America in order to raise money for the creation of an Irish Academy of Letters which he, with Shaw and AE, had founded that year. *Riversdale* Yeats and his family had now left Dublin and had moved to a house called 'Riversdale', near Rathfarnham, a village that lies between the city of Dublin and the mountains. This was to be his last home in Ireland. The years that followed were to be good years for him, living with his wife, son and daughter in that early nineteenth-century house and its gardens where 'plum and cabbage grew' – a house where, happy and at peace for a while, considering himself at last a settled man, he had about him 'many birds'. He continued to write with undiminished energy and brilliance. In 1933 *The Winding Stair and other Poems*, and a new edition

Yeats in 1930

◀ 'Riversdale', Rathfarnham, near Dublin, Yeats' last home in Ireland.

Friends of Yeats during his later years. (*Left*) Ethel Mannin.
(*Below*) Oliver St John Gogarty. (*Opposite*) Edith and
Osbert Sitwell

of his *Collected Poems*, were published; in 1934 his *Collected Plays* appeared. Dublin friends gathered about him – Frank O'Connor, Cecil Salkeld, Arland Usher, and the poet F. R. Higgins – and he paid frequent visits to London, where he was welcomed by Ezra Pound, Ethel Mannin, the Sitwells, and Dorothy Wellesley, who remained a close friend to the end of his life. Was it perhaps Lady Dorothy who inspired him to flirt for a while with the ideology of fascism? This was a bias born of his instinctive love for old tradition, for a dream almost feudal in its conception that led many people to doubt his political wisdom.

In 1934, as Dr Oliver St John Gogarty has recalled, 'Yeats' disdain for science led him into what was a singular experiment. It left him open to the highly-coloured claims of rejuvenating operations. . . . I was horrified to hear,' Dr Gogarty adds, 'when it was too late, that he had undergone such an operation.' So it was, and inevitably with Yeats, as would be the case with any dedicated artist, the experiment that was primarily physical in nature manifested itself by casting a strange new light over his vision of life, over his imagination, over the matter and manner of his work. 'Lust and rage,' as he cried out in a brief and half-resentful apologia for the new, unwonted spirit that flowed through him, were 'dancing attendance' on his declining years. They had not been 'such a plague' in his youth, he declared, and he demanded, with a certain bitter challenge, what else had he to spur him to the labour of song. Poems like those in the sequence called *A Woman Young and Old*, and like 'The Statues' and 'News for the Delphic Oracle' in *Last Poems*, reflect this mood of violent yet still shadow-haunted sensuality where

> *Nymphs and satyrs*
> *Copulate in the foam.*

His whole being at these moments becomes like a town in the grip of alien occupation. It is as though Hecate and Aphrodite, a whole multitude of frenzied Bacchantes at their heels, had alighted on the thrones of Niamh (the beloved shadow who enchanted Oisín), and of Éimear the faithful wife of Cú Chulainn, and of the phantom Hosts who rode the air about them; and those people who had loved the almost bodiless passions of his earlier dreams were half startled, half saddened by the transformation.

Side by side with this insistent eroticism there appeared for the first time in Yeats' personality, and in those occasional works in which Hecate and Aphrodite seem for a while to lie asleep in his blood, that odd 'voluminous tenderness' that he himself had once described as being characteristic of the voluptuary. He seems at such moments of peace to have turned his eyes away from the darkness into which he had looked for so long, being certain, as he had said, that 'when one looks into darkness there is always something there'. At times, too, he could turn from his preoccupation with sexual desire to the memory of old, tranquil friendships, untroubled by any passion but that of some shared ideal. He recalls comrades of the Rhymers' Club at the Cheshire Cheese during the nineties, and memories of old, gracious country houses with flowering lawns. A visit to the Dublin Municipal Galleries revives for him, as he looks at certain portraits on the walls, thoughts of John Synge and many others; of all

> *My permanent or impermanent images:*
> *Augusta Gregory's son; her sister's son,*
> *Hugh Lane, 'onlie begetter' of all these;*
> *Hazel Lavery living and dying, that tale*
> *As though some ballad-singer had sung it all.*

Age, in fact, was approaching, and with it, inevitably, some little share of tranquillity, in spite of the rejuvenating experiment that had set his blood on fire. Yet the old restlessness, the insatiable curiosity, the always unexpected pugnacity, were still with him and remained with him to the end.

110

Major Robert Gregory (Lady Gregory's son), by Charles Shannon. Gregory was killed in action over Italy in 1917, while serving in the Royal Flying Corps. Yeats wrote several poems in his memory, 'An Irish Airman Foresees his Death' being the most famous

Manuscript of 'An Irish Airman Foresees his Death'

on the death of an Irish air-man
who joined early in the war

" I know that I shall meet my fate
Somewhere among the clouds above,
Those that I fight I do not hate
Those that I guard I do not love.
My country is Kiltartan Cross
my countrys men Kiltartans poor
no likely end can bring them loss
or leave them happier then before.
nor law, no duty bade me fight
nor public men nor angry crowd
a lonely impulse of delight
Drove to this tumult in the clouds.
I balanced all brought all to mind
The years to come seemed waste of breath
a waste of breath the years behind
In ballance with this life or death

'Homage to Sir Hugh Lane', by J. Keating. Sir Hugh Lane, the art collector, played an important part in the foundation of the Municipal Gallery of Modern Art in Dublin in 1908. From left to right: Yeats, Dermod O'Brien, Thomas Bodkin, A E (George Russell), W. Hutchinson-Poe, Thomas Kelly, R. Caulfield-Orpen

His admiration for Lady Dorothy Wellesley and for her poetry helped to strengthen his instinctive love of brilliant and distinguished people, of the ancient traditions of noble families: almost of the sacred right of kings. It helped to cause that romantic sublimation of a certain *folie de grandeur* which had always lived at the back of his mind. The respectability of the Yeats family, so much admired by the Sligo barber of earlier days, had now been transmuted in the poet's mind into something far more significant. His growing affection for his forebears, his half-stated claims to some nobility of lineage, may conceivably be linked, paradoxically enough, with his belief in reincarnation. Was this longing for ancestors a reflection of the search in his imagination for an ancestry of the soul which might, indeed, have yielded a forebear of himself who would have been formidable enough to satisfy his wildest hopes? Why should he, who cared for nothing but spiritual and intellectual perfection, bother his head about whether the Butlers in his family were Ormonde Butlers or not? He who had so often quoted the phrase, 'the spirit bloweth where it listeth', should have remembered that supreme ability may arise from the most opposed of physiologically traceable sources, its true origins being beyond discovery by science. Sophocles and Count Tolstoy came from distinguished families, but Shakespeare and Keats were born into humble homes. Lord Byron and Alexander Pushkin were aristocrats; but Leonardo was the illegitimate son of a notary and a peasant girl. The social rank of the forebears of great men seems to be of little reliable significance. Was not Buddha a prince, and Jesus of Nazareth a carpenter?

Interest in ancestry

All through these declining years Yeats' mind and his spirit, like his body, were informed by an inner turbulence, a restless and indefinably tragic violence. Yet although both his verse and his prose manifested an astonishing revolution in style, much of his subject matter remained unaltered. It is noteworthy that his brother, Jack Butler Yeats, who had undergone no rejuvenating operation, nevertheless showed a similar change in the style of his painting after his sixtieth year, retaining, in a parallel fashion, much of the imagery and background of his earlier pictures. In the painter's later work we are still in the visible world of the west of Ireland, still among stormy skies and seas and rain-shrouded mountains; we see these, however, through eyes which have grown wild, not with the capricious energy of youth, but with the savage tenacity of age. A rout of new images intrudes: suddenly, in place of hills and bogs and the snugs of country taverns among itinerants and cutters of turf, we find ourselves in city streets or theatres or in some great room full of books, and strange or familiar urban faces gaze at us through a glittering light. In his brother's poetry and poetic plays there is a like sequence of background, of landscape, of settled individuality of geography; but the mood has changed startlingly, the characters have a new and unfamiliar identity. Now it is Dean Swift and the learned Berkeley who pass across the scene in place of Maeve and Goll Mac Morna,

Style of last works

Lough Gill, and the lake island of Innisfree, County Sligo

I will arise and go now, and go to Innisfree,
And a small cabin build there, of clay and wattles made:
Nine bean-rows will I have there, a hive for the honey-bee,
And live alone in the bee-loud glade.

◄   *(On the previous two pages)* Ben Bulben, from West Glencar

Knocknarea, County Sligo, a drawing made from the lawn at Lissadell House
The host is riding from Knocknarea
And over the grave of Clooth-na-Bare;
Caoilte tossing his burning hair,
And Niamh calling Away, come away.

now Crazy Jane and the Roaring Tinker who rise before us like lean phantoms battered by the wind. It is as though we were watching Shakespearean drama acted by a constantly changing cast against a setting of whose permanence we are only half aware, so great a spell the play of shifting lights and shadows has cast upon us. For although Jane and Tinker and Hudden and Dudden and Tim the Lunatic ride the same mountains which the lordly ones of the Sidhe have haunted (does not Crazy Jane see Cú Chulainn pass by with 'great-bladdered Emer' at his side?), we seem at other times to be watching a lamp-lit library where learned Irish gentlemen of the eighteenth century sit, and the midnight bells chime in the darkness beyond the windows.

No writer's life had been more dedicated than Yeats', more outwardly uneventful or more inwardly teeming with energy, with what he would have loved to believe – and, who knows? he may have been right – was some joyous, supernatural power. His nature, as he remarked, was sedentary and thoughtful; he travelled but seldom, and little if anything can be traced in his story that could conceivably interest lovers of the sensational. It was not only the years of his twenties that were 'crammed with toil', as he wrote in 'What then?'. This poem (from *Last Poems*) is as significant as it is surprising, for it reads like the confession of a man who felt that nothing that he had done was of any lasting value; an uneasy conscience, like that of some remorse-ful lotus-eater, seems to be mocking his impotence with the voice of Plato. (Each

117

verse concludes with the refrain, '"What then?" sang Plato's ghost, "What then?"'.) Yet what artist or saint or statesman laboured more than Yeats? What greater fulfilment could he have attained? He had, as he quietly observed in the same poem, everything that should have made him contented; yet the ghostly Platonic voice continued to ignore all that had been done, to spur him on, like a relentless taskmaster, to more and more labour. Was it the same voice that in childhood, even when he thought of God, had tormented him with the conviction of his own wickedness?

Remembering his middle and last years – the golden beauty of 'Sailing to Byzantium', the splendour of 'Under Ben Bulben' with its changing rhythms and the noble austerity of its final message of farewell – remembering too the monumental quality of his best achievements and rewards, the student of Yeats' life and work is puzzled again and again by one thought. It is this: as his writing grew more perfect, his influence, outside the little, sacred, intense world of poetry, grew less and less. For it was not the Senator, nor the impressive aesthete and social figure, nor the winner of the Nobel Prize, nor the authority on Dean Swift and on the theory of magic – nor even the acknowledged major poet of the English-speaking world of his day – that cast a spell over Ireland and Ireland's spell over the world. The *Yeats' influence* nature of Yeats' incalculable influence on the intellectual and national destinies of his compatriots had been decided long ago by the lanky youth who wandered alone over the Sligo roads and by the lakes and raths of Galway. During this century, there has been no Irishman or woman in the world of literature or of the theatre who has not followed at one time or another the way his vague, impractical finger pointed to – from Colum to Joyce, from Beckett to Kate O'Brien. The intellectual Ireland of today was conceived in the minds of two men, Douglas Hyde and William Butler Yeats, as political Ireland was conceived in the minds of the men who created Sinn Féin and of those who signed the Republican Proclamation of the Easter Rising in 1916. Both aspects of modern Ireland, of course, had far more ancient roots, roots that are indeed as old as the land itself; but these were the men who bade them continue to grow. Ireland has developed in a manner far removed from the original dreams in the minds of Yeats and Douglas Hyde on the one hand; in the minds of Arthur Griffith and Pádraic Pearse on the other. The Ireland of today would at once astonish them and, in many ways, disappoint them. Yet it is largely their creation. Coming at his own particular moment in history, Yeats, perhaps more than any of his contemporaries, wielded an only half-understood influence that should make his name as significant in the history of the Irish imagination and its utterance as that of Pushkin is in the imaginative history of Russia.

In the mid-1930s Yeats was still to be seen at the Abbey Theatre, both in the stalls and back-stage: an imposing, restless figure. Few except his intimate friends guessed at the decline of his bodily health: he appeared to be continually urged

Yeats during his last years

Mrs Patrick Campbell
in the title part of
Deirdre (a production
in 1908)

forward by a violent mental and physical energy. His powers were still journeying
from one experiment to another, from one adventure to another, still making new
discoveries. The present writer, receiving from him in 1935 a letter of praise for a
performance of Naoise in a revival of his play *Deirdre*, was surprised by the phrase,
'Now that I am but a ghost I can speak the truth.' The remark seemed at the time to
Health worsens   be simply an echo of the impressive image of Yeats' earlier self. Yet it was true
enough, for with the return of the lung congestion which had first begun to afflict
him in 1927, the condition of the poet's health was now growing serious. Nevertheless, he continued to be very active. In 1935 the collection of poems *From 'A Full
Moon in March'* was published, and Yeats began work on editing *The Oxford Book of
Modern Verse*, which was published in the following year. His long introduction to
this anthology showed no sign at all of fading powers. His choice of poetry has been

The harbour of Palma, Majorca. Yeats stayed in Majorca from the winter of 1935 until the spring of 1936

much criticized; for instance, he included eight pages of lyrics by Oliver St John Gogarty, but totally omitted Wilfred Owen, Lord Alfred Douglas and many other distinguished poets. (As might be expected, Lord Alfred Douglas was furious at being excluded, and never forgave Yeats to the end of his days.) Controversial though it is, *The Oxford Book of Modern Verse* does throw much light on Yeats' personality and literary ideals.

Meanwhile, a meeting with the Indian mystic Shri Purohit Swami had re-kindled in him his passion for Eastern religions and philosophy. In the winter of 1935 the two men – Irish poet and Indian sage – went to Majorca together and *Majorca* planned there a new English translation of the Upanishads. Yeats remained in Majorca until the spring of 1936. From now onwards Ireland was to see him only in summer-time. In 1936 and 1937 he delivered broadcast lectures on poetry for the

121

Yeats giving a
broadcast in a B.B.C.
studio

B.B.C. and made recordings of his own verse. He spent the winter of 1937–38 in
Menton, where, forty years before, his young friend Aubrey Beardsley had died.
During 1938 Yeats wrote a one-act play, *Purgatory*. He was present at the first performance, which took place at the Abbey Theatre in August, and spoke to the
audience from the stage for what was to be the last time. The same year brought one
final sadness to Yeats; Olivia Shakespear died in London. Yeats wrote of her with
his customary grace in a letter to Dorothy Wellesley: 'For more than forty years she
has been the centre of my life in London, and during all that time we have never had
a quarrel, sadness sometimes, but never a difference.'

Towards the close of 1938 Mrs Yeats brought her husband to stay in an hotel at
Cap Martin in the Alpes Maritimes, where her care and companionship, the beauty
of sea and sky and mountains, the radiance of the sun and the presence of a few
friends made his last days far happier than those of many poets and artists. A tranquillity, even a gaiety of spirit were with him. In a letter to a friend written two weeks
before his death he made it clear that he was conscious that his time on earth would
not be long, adding that he was content: 'I am happy, and I think full of an energy,
of an energy I had despaired of. It seems to me that I have found what I wanted.
When I try to put all into a phrase, I say, "Man can embody truth, but he cannot
know it."'

Death   Yeats died of heart-failure on 28 January 1939, at the age of seventy-three, and
was buried in the little cemetery at Rocquebrune, the village that hangs in the

Roquebrune, Alpes Maritimes, France, where Yeats was buried

Yeats' coffin outside the Chapel of St Pancrace, Roquebrune,
before it was taken to Ireland for interment at Drumcliff,
County Sligo. On the left is Marius Otto, a local poet who
composed and read a funeral poem in memory of Yeats

sunlight under the high mountains and over the sea between Monaco and Menton.
In 1948 his body was brought ceremoniously back to Ireland and was interred, as
he had wished, under the shadow of Ben Bulben in the earth of Drumcliff in the
County Sligo, between the mountains and the road winding by the western sea,
northward to Donegal, southward to Knocknarea. In accordance with the wishes
expressed by him in 'Under Ben Bulben', the gravestone bears this inscription:

> Cast a cold eye
> On life, on death.
> Horseman, pass by!

Yeats' character In his manner to strangers he was courteous, stately and formal; at times he
seemed remote, behind a mask of exaggerated dignity. With people whom he liked
and felt he understood he would unbend and become by turns eloquent, turbulent
and laughing. But never, as far as the present writer can remember, was there any
humorous warmth of intimacy in his demeanour. All that he did or said had an air
of ceremony; one could not imagine him engaged in shopping, or mending the
fire, or taking an inquiring stranger by the arm and showing him the quickest way
to O'Connell Street, though he himself might ask the way in a voice which sug-
gested that he spoke from a great distance. Yeats (at times, one suspects, with his
tongue delicately tipped towards his cheek) would give dignity and intellectual

The re-interment of Yeats' coffin at Drumcliff in 1948 (Yeats' son is second from the left, his widow third from the left), and (*right*) Yeats' grave at Drumcliff

weight to the flightiest things; there was a gravity, an almost ecclesiastical ritualism, about the way in which he signed a cheque or put on his overcoat, and he would order a waiter to bring him a mutton chop in the tones of one who seeks the Holy Grail. Soon after his first shave, he spread about him an atmosphere of lofty aloofness and solitude, although, even in his early days in Rathgar, he was already surrounded by friends and supporters. He loved to quote what he called Villiers de l'Isle-Adam's proud cry, 'As for living, our servants will do that for us', and he seemed to carry the conviction into daily life.

Always the hawk was present in his personality. He would seem to float in his conversation among distant clouds, and then suddenly to pounce on an adversary with a brief, newly discovered phrase; always he was unexpected. Dublin, of course, was full of stories about his eccentricities. He once borrowed a pair of scissors from the Abbey Theatre's wardrobe mistress and with it cut away half of a new fur coat, rather than disturb the theatre cat who lay asleep on the coat where he had left it on a sofa in the green-room. 'The cat,' he observed, explaining the reason for his abbreviated coat, 'was, I believe, in a magical sleep: it would have been dangerous to wake her.' On another occasion, when attending to some business that demanded his name on many cheques, he signed them all, 'Yours sincerely, W. B. Yeats'. Again, while talking with rapt eloquence about his theory of the Phases of the Moon over a cup of tea, he broke off in the middle of an elaborately mystical phrase

125

Yeats, a portrait bust by Albert Power

to say to his companion, 'Longford, you are drinking from my cup!' Once more the hawk had swept down upon its prey.

And Dublin, more than any other city, mocked at him with Dublin's special brand of light-hearted malice and called him 'That fella' and 'Willy the Spooks' and 'The Gland Old Man'. Ireland has always laughed at its distinguished men and women, and it will take far greater upheavals than the nation has yet known to induce it to change its ways. Yet, with all its mockery of the poet, all its derision, all its accusations of oddity, of wilful obscurity, and of the element of *poseur* in the complexity of his personality, it would be impossible to imagine any more complete gift to a nation so sorely in need of gifts than the dedication of the life and work of Yeats to his country. And that the gift which he brought was fraught with mystery and strangeness does not lessen its immeasurable value. We may be reminded of a man bringing frankincense and myrrh to some stricken house where nothing but bread is asked for, but we must be filled with wonder at the casket of ivory and gold laid at the feet of poverty, and at the magical things which it contains. The gift and the giver were, of course, suspected by many. 'Heresy', was whispered in some quarters; 'Pose and tomfoolery', in others. It was thought during his life-time, and the thought is still alive today – especially, oddly enough, among his admirers – that the supernatural beliefs that permeate his work were adopted merely as an attitude, or that, at best, they represent an awkward and inexplicable gap in a mind otherwise brilliantly equipped. 'Had he his tongue in his cheek when he wrote all that nonsense?' is a phrase which sums up this point of view as well as another. But in truth it was not so. Yeats' belief in 'that nonsense' was the most fundamental thing in his nature: it was at least as passionate and unshakable as the faith of any devout Christian, Buddhist, Jew or Mohammedan, if a little more restless in its search for some permanent shape. That restlessness was the proof of his sincerity. Indeed, so deep was his need for the presence of that other invisible life brooding over the life which he knew, that it was through it, I believe, that he discovered the urge to serve his own country. His conviction that Ireland had preserved 'among other less admirable things', as he wrote in a letter to AE, 'a gift of vision' was what led him to his national bias.

It was fortunate for Ireland herself that this was so, and fortunate too, for Ireland and for literature, that he never swerved from his central idea. In his introduction to the *Oxford Book of Modern Verse*, he wrote, after analyzing the poetry of the 1890s, 'Then in 1900 everybody got down off his stilts: henceforth nobody drank absinthe with his black coffee; nobody went mad; nobody committed suicide; nobody joined the Catholic Church; or if they did I have forgotten.'

With what unutterable pleasure and gratitude may it be observed that the Irish poet once again proved the exception to a rule. Never for one moment of his life did Yeats get down off his stilts.

The churchyard at Drumcliff. Ben Bulben can be seen in the background

BIBLIOGRAPHICAL NOTE

A comprehensive bibliography of Yeats' own works is *A Bibliography of the Writings of W.B. Yeats*, by Allan Wade; the third edition, revised and edited by Russell K. Alspach, was published in London in 1968. A good list of books and articles about Yeats, and of the most important critical studies of his poems, is *Prolegomena to the Study of Yeats' Poems*, by George Brandon Saul (Philadelphia, 1957). The most useful editions of Yeats' writings, and a selection of the most important books about him and his work, are listed below.

Yeats revised many of his poems and plays after they had appeared in print. Readers who wish to compare the final versions (given in the collected editions of the poems and plays mentioned below) with the original published texts will find the following two books invaluable: *The Variorum Edition of the Poems of W.B. Yeats*, edited by Peter Allt and Russell K. Alspach (New York, 1957), and *The Variorum Edition of the Plays of W.B. Yeats*, edited by Russell K. Alspach, assisted by Catherine C. Alspach (London, 1966).

The quotations from Yeats' poetry in the present work have been taken from the second edition of *The Collected Poems of W.B. Yeats*, mentioned below.

EDITIONS OF YEATS' WORKS

The Collected Poems of W.B. Yeats, second edition, with later poems added (London, 1950)
The Collected Plays of W.B. Yeats, second edition, with additional plays (London, 1952)
Autobiographies, consisting of 'Reveries over Childhood and Youth', 'The Trembling of the Veil', 'Dramatis Personae', 'Estrangement', 'The Death of Synge' and 'The Bounty of Sweden' (London, 1955)
Essays and Introductions (London, 1961)
A Vision, second edition, reissued with corrections (London, 1962)
The Letters of W.B. Yeats, edited by Allan Wade (London, 1954)

BOOKS ABOUT YEATS

Ellmann, Richard, *The Identity of Yeats* (London, 1954)
Ellmann, Richard, *Yeats. The Man and the Masks* (London, 1949)
Henn, T.R., *The Lonely Tower. Studies in the Poetry of W.B. Yeats*, second edition, revised and enlarged (London, 1965)
Hone, Joseph M., *W.B. Yeats, 1865–1939* (the standard biography; London, 1942)
Jeffares, A. Norman, *W.B. Yeats. Man and Poet*, second edition (London, 1962)
Jeffares, A. Norman, *A Commentary on the Collected Poems of W.B. Yeats* (London, 1968)
Stauffer, Donald A., *The Golden Nightingale. Essays on some Principles of Poetry in the Lyrics of William Butler Yeats* (New York, 1949)

CHRONOLOGY

1865 William Butler Yeats born in Sandy-mount, Dublin, on 13 June, the son of John Butler Yeats, painter, and Susan Yeats, *née* Pollexfen.

1868 Family moves to 23 Fitzroy Road, Regent's Park, London.

1874 Family moves to 14 Edith Villas, West Kensington. Yeats begins to attend the Godolphin School, Hammersmith.

1876 Family moves to Bedford Park.

1880 Family returns to Ireland, settling at Howth.

1881 Yeats starts to attend Erasmus High School, Dublin.

1882 Yeats writes his earliest poetry.

1883 Family moves to 10 Ashfield Terrace, Rathgar, Dublin.

1884 Yeats starts to attend the Metropolitan School of Art, Dublin, where his father is a master. Meets AE (George Russell).

1885 Two poems (Yeats' earliest published verse) appear in the *Dublin University Review*. Yeats meets John O'Leary.

1886 Yeats leaves the Metropolitan School of Art. *Mosada* published in Dublin.

1887 Family moves to England, living first at 58 Eardley Crescent, Earl's Court, London. 'The Madness of King Goll' (Yeats' first poem to be published in England) appears in *The Leisure Hour*.

1888 Family now living at 3 Blenheim Road, Bedford Park. Yeats completes *The Wanderings of Oisin* at the house of his uncle, George Pollexfen, in Sligo.

1889 *The Wanderings of Oisin and other Poems* published. Yeats meets Maud Gonne.

1890 Yeats joins the Hermetic Order of the Golden Dawn.

1891 Yeats, Ernest Rhys and T. W. Rolleston found the Rhymers' Club in London. Yeats founds the Irish Literary Society (London). Proposes to Maud Gonne, who refuses him. Writes *The Countess Cathleen*. Charles Stewart Parnell dies on 11 October.

1892 Yeats founds the Irish Literary Society (Dublin). *The Countess Cathleen and Various Legends and Lyrics* published.

1894 *The Land of Heart's Desire* produced in London.

1896 Yeats moves to rooms in Woburn Buildings. Meets Lady Gregory at Edward Martyn's house in County Galway. Meets J. M. Synge in Paris.

1899   The first plays produced by the Irish Literary Theatre, *The Countess Cathleen* and Edward Martyn's *The Heather Field*, performed at the Antient Concert Rooms, Dublin. *The Wind among the Reeds* published.

1902   *Cathleen ni Houlihan* produced in Dublin, with Maud Gonne in the title part. The Irish Literary Theatre replaced by the Irish National Theatre, of which Yeats becomes president.

1903   Miss A. E. Horniman offers to build and equip a new theatre for the Irish National Theatre. Maud Gonne marries Major John MacBride. *In the Seven Woods* (poems), *Baile and Aillin* (narrative poem) and *Ideas of Good and Evil* (essays) published.

1904   The Abbey Theatre built, under Miss Horniman's patronage, in Abbey Street, Dublin; it opens in December with the first productions of Yeats' *On Baile's Strand* and Lady Gregory's *Spreading the News*.

1905   *The Shadowy Waters* produced in London.

1906   *The Shadowy Waters* (revised version) published.

1907   J. M. Synge's *The Playboy of the Western World* produced at the Abbey Theatre. Yeats' first visit to Italy.

1909   J. M. Synge dies on 24 March.

1910   Yeats is granted a Civil List pension. *The Green Helmet and other Poems* published. Miss Horniman withdraws her financial support from the Abbey Theatre.

1911   Yeats meets George Hyde-Lees, his future wife.

1914   *Responsibilities* published.

1916   The rising of the Irish Republican volunteers takes place on Easter Monday, 24 April. Major MacBride tried and executed for his participation.

1917   Yeats marries George Hyde-Lees in London on 21 October.

1918   The Yeatses settle in a house in Broad Street, Oxford, then move to Dublin. *Per Amica Silentia Lunae* published.

1919   A daughter, Anne, born to the Yeatses on 24 February. They move into 'Thoor Ballylee', County Galway, and in October travel to the United States, where Yeats begins a lecture tour. *The Wild Swans at Coole* published.

1920   Lecture tour ends in May. The Yeatses return to England, settling in Oxford.

1921   A son, Michael, born to the Yeatses on 22 August at Thame. The Irish Free State established on 6 December. *Michael Robartes and the Dancer* published.

1922   Outbreak of the Irish Civil War. The Yeatses move to 82 Merrion Square, Dublin.

1923   Yeats takes up seat in the Irish Senate on 13 January. The Civil War ends during the summer. Yeats is awarded the Nobel Prize for Literature, and receives the Diploma and Medal from the King of Sweden in Stockholm on 10 December.

1925   *A Vision* published.

1926   Yeats' translation of Sophocles' *Oedipus the King* produced at the Abbey Theatre.

1927   Yeats' translation of Sophocles' *Oedipus at Colonus* produced at the Abbey

Theatre. After an attack of lung congestion Yeats, to recover his health, travels first to Spain (staying at Algeciras and Seville) and then to the French Riviera (staying at Cannes).

1928 In February the Yeatses move from Cannes to Rapallo. *The Tower* published. In April the Yeatses travel to Ireland. Yeats gives his last speech in the Senate on 18 July; does not seek re-election. The Yeatses return to Rapallo for the winter.

1929 The Yeatses travel to Ireland in the spring; visit 'Thoor Ballylee' for the last time in the summer. *A Packet for Ezra Pound* published. *Fighting the Waves* (one of the 'Plays for Dancers') produced at the Abbey Theatre by Ninette de Valois. The Yeatses return to Rapallo for the winter.

1930 *The Words upon the Window Pane* produced at the Abbey Theatre. Yeats spends the winter at Lady Gregory's house (Coole Park, County Galway), where she is seriously ill.

1931 Yeats receives honorary degree of Doctor of Letters from Oxford University in May. Spends the winter at Coole Park.

1932 Lady Gregory dies on 22 May. Yeats, George Bernard Shaw and AE found the Irish Academy of Letters. In October Yeats undertakes a lecture tour of America.

1933 The Yeatses now living at 'Riversdale', Rathfarnham, near Dublin. *The Winding Stair and other Poems* published.

1935 AE dies. *From 'A Full Moon in March'* published. In the winter Yeats travels to Majorca with Shri Purohit Swami to plan translation of the Upanishads.

1936 Yeats seriously ill in Majorca during January; his wife joins him. The Yeatses return to 'Riversdale' in June. *The Oxford Book of Modern Verse* (edited by Yeats) published. Yeats writes the earliest of the poems published posthumously in *Last Poems* (1940). Broadcasts a lecture on poetry on the B.B.C. on 20 October.

1937 Yeats broadcasts four further lectures on poetry on the B.B.C. The Yeatses move to Menton for the winter.

1938 Yeats travels to Ireland in May, then spends part of the summer in England. Makes his last public appearance at the first performance of *Purgatory* at the Abbey Theatre in August. Olivia Shakespear dies. Yeats prepares prose draft of his last play, *The Death of Cuchulain*, in London on the way to the French Riviera, where he and his wife take rooms at the Hôtel Idéal Séjour, Cap Martin.

1939 Yeats dies on 28 January at Cap Martin, and is buried on 31 January at Roquebrune.

1948 Yeats' body is brought to Ireland and re-interred at Drumcliff, County Sligo.

133

NOTES ON THE PICTURES

The details between square brackets indicate the sources of the quotations given in the captions, which are from Yeats' own writings unless it is stated otherwise

Frontispiece: W.B. YEATS photographed by Hoppé. *Photo Mansell Collection.*

5 DRUMCLIFF, County Sligo. The church and churchyard. *Photo National Gallery of Ireland.*

6 JOHN BUTLER YEATS. A self-portrait. *Photo National Gallery of Ireland. Collection Senator M. Yeats.*

SUSAN YEATS (née Pollexfen). Painting by John Butler Yeats. *Photo National Gallery of Ireland.*

7 SLIGO. St John's Church is in the foreground. *Photo Irish Tourist Board.*

8 JACK B. YEATS (1871–1957). Painting of him as a boy by John Butler Yeats. Ireland's greatest painter, Jack B. Yeats devoted his art to rendering the Irish themselves, especially the country people both at work and at leisure: fishermen, bargees, jockeys, boxers, fairground audiences. He also showed an original literary talent in his plays (*Apparations* and *La La Noo*) and in his prose writings (*Sligo, The Amaranthers, The Careless Flower*). *Photo National Gallery of Ireland.*

9 SIR JOHN POYNTER, R.A. *Photo Mansell Collection.*

10 YEATS, 1907. Etching by Augustus John. *Photo National Portrait Gallery, London.*

11 GEORGE POLLEXFEN. Painting by John Butler Yeats. *Photo National Gallery of Ireland. Collection Senator M. Yeats.* ['In Memory of Major Robert Gregory', V, 1–3.]

13 'GEORGEVILLE', 5 Sandymount Avenue, Dublin. Yeats' birthplace. Drawing by W.G. Spencer. *Photo R.B. Fleming and Co. Ltd.*

23 FITZROY ROAD, Regent's Park, London. *Photo David Eccles.*

14 SLIGO. The harbour. *Photo Irish Tourist Board.* ['The Meditation of the Old Fisherman', 6–8.]

15 GLENCAR LAKE. *Photo Irish Tourist Board.* ['The Tower', I, 9–11.]

16 ELIZABETH C. YEATS ('Lolly'). Painting by John Butler Yeats. *Photo National Gallery of Ireland. Collection Senator M. Yeats.*

LILY (SUSAN) YEATS. Painting by John Butler Yeats. *Photo National Gallery of Ireland.*

17 THE GODOLPHIN SCHOOL (now the Godolphin and Latymer School), Hammersmith, in 1862. From the *Illustrated London News*, April 1862. *Photo Libraries Department, London Borough of Hammersmith.*

18 YEATS as a boy. Sketch by John Butler Yeats. *Photo National Library of Ireland.*

19 WOODSTOCK ROAD, Bedford Park, London. *Photo David Eccles.*

20 ERASMUS HIGH SCHOOL, Harcourt Street, Dublin. Architect's drawing.

21 HOWTH, County Dublin. *Photo Edwin Smith.*

22 HOWTH, the bay and cliffs. *Photo Irish Tourist Board.*

ST STEPHEN'S GREEN, DUBLIN. *Photo Mansell Collection.*

23 YEATS as a young man. Photographed by Hollyer. *Photo Radio Times Hulton Picture Library.*

24 AE, the pen-name of GEORGE W. RUSSELL (1867–1935). Poet, essayist, journalist, social thinker and painter, AE was a major force in the Irish literary revival. He was a theosophist, and his poetry is mystical in character. He was an economist who believed that England and Ireland were economically dependent on each other; for this reason, though an ardent nationalist, he did not take part in the Easter Rising of 1916. He was editor of *The Irish Statesman*, 1923–30. *Photo Radio Times Hulton Picture Library.*

YEATS. Drawing (1903) by AE. *Photo National Gallery of Ireland.*

25 JOHN O'LEARY. Photograph taken in 1894 by T. W. Rolleston. *Photo courtesy Lady Albery.* ['September 1913', last two lines of first three stanzas.]

26 DOUGLAS HYDE (1860–1949). Painting by John Butler Yeats. A literary scholar who played an important part in the Irish literary revival, Hyde was the author of books in Irish and in English, including *The Story of Early Gaelic Literature* (1895) and *Literary History of Ireland* (1899). He also published volumes of folk stories and folk-poetry (notably *Love Songs of Connacht*, which contains his own verse translations from the Irish). Hyde became the first President of Eire in 1937. *Photo Municipal Gallery of Modern Art, Dublin.*

27 KATHARINE TYNAN. Painting by John Butler Yeats. *Photo Municipal Gallery of Modern Art, Dublin.*

28 EARDLEY CRESCENT, Earl's Court, London. *Photo David Eccles.*

BLENHEIM ROAD, Bedford Park, London. *Photo David Eccles.*

29 MADAME BLAVATSKY. *Photo courtesy the Theosophical Society in England.*

30 MADAME BLAVATSKY'S HOUSE, Lansdowne Road, London: the living room. *Photo courtesy the Theosophical Society in England.*

31 GEORGE BERNARD SHAW. Photograph taken in about 1890. *Photo Radio Times Hulton Picture Library.*

OSCAR WILDE. Photograph taken in 1894. *Photo Radio Times Hulton Picture Library.*

32 W.E. HENLEY. *Photo Radio Times Hulton Picture Library.*

WILLIAM MORRIS. Sketch by John Butler Yeats made at the Contemporary Club, 116 Grafton Street, Dublin, where Morris lectured. *Photo National Gallery of Ireland.*

33 ROSSES POINT, County Sligo. *Photo Irish Tourist Board.* ['The Stolen Child', II, 1–4.]

Notes

35 GLENCAR WATERFALL, County Sligo. *Photo Irish Tourist Board.* ['The Stolen Child', III, 1–4.]

36 EDWARD DOWDEN. *Photo Radio Times Hulton Picture Library.*

37 CARTOON ON THE COERCION ACT. From an issue of the *Dublin Evening Telegraph*, 1889. British Museum, Department of Prints and Drawings. *Photo Freeman.*

39 MAUD GONNE. Painting by Sarah Purser. *Photo Municipal Gallery of Modern Art, Dublin.* ['The Folly of being Comforted', 9–12.]

40 ERNEST RHYS (1859–1946). Original photograph by Hollyer. Rhys published two volumes of poetry and two volumes of autobiography, but is best known as the founder of 'Everyman's Library'. *Photo courtesy Stephen Rhys.*

41 FLEET STREET, London, in about 1900. Original photograph by F. J. Mortimer. *Photo Radio Times Hulton Picture Library.* ['Coole Park and Ballylee, 1931', VI, 1–2.]

42 T. W. ROLLESTON. *Photo courtesy Lady Albery.*

43 YEATS. Original photograph by T. W. Rolleston, November 1894. *Photo courtesy Lady Albery.*

44 'SOME PERSONS OF THE 90S'. Cartoon by Sir Max Beerbohm, 1925. *Photo courtesy the Ashmolean Museum, Oxford.*

46 'THE COUNTESS CATHLEEN'. The jacket of the first edition (1892).

47 MAUD GONNE. *Photo courtesy Victor Gollancz Ltd.* ['Fallen Majesty', II.]

48 CHARLES STEWART PARNELL. Painting (1892) by Sydney Prior Hall. *Photo National Gallery of Ireland.* ['Come Gather round me, Parnellites', II, 3–4.]

KITTY O'SHEA. *Photo Radio Times Hulton Picture Library.*

49 'THE SAVOY'. Cover, with an illustration by Aubrey Beardsley, July 1896. British Museum, Department of Printed Books. *Photo Freeman.*

50 ARTHUR WILLIAM SYMONS (1865–1945). Photograph taken at St John's Wood, 22 September 1906. Poet, playwright and critic, Symons was a major figure in the English literary world of the 1890s and a member of the Rhymers' Club. An authority on contemporary French literature, he published *The Symbolist Movement in Literature* (1899), as well as translations from several foreign languages. He strongly supported his friend Yeats in the struggle to win appreciation in England for the achievements of the Irish literary revival. *Photo Radio Times Hulton Picture Library.*

51 'THE TOILET OF HELEN'. From *Under the Hill*, by Aubrey Beardsley.

AUBREY BEARDSLEY. Painting by W. R. Sickert. *Photo Tate Gallery.*

52 OLIVIA SHAKESPEAR. *Photo courtesy Rupert Hart-Davis Ltd.*

53 MAUD GONNE. Photograph taken in 1897. *Photo National Library of Ireland.* ['A Woman Homer Sung', III.]

55 WOBURN PLACE, off Russell Square, London. *Photo David Eccles.*

56 'THE LAND OF HEART'S DESIRE'. Poster by Aubrey Beardsley announcing the

first performance. *Photo Abbey Theatre, Dublin.*

WINIFRED FRASER AND DOROTHY PAGET in *The Land of Heart's Desire. Photo courtesy Mander and Mitchenson Theatre Collection.*

57 FLORENCE FARR. *Photo courtesy Routledge and Kegan Paul Ltd.*

58 EDWARD MARTYN. Painting by Sarah Purser. Martyn, a rich landlord, provided the initial financial support for the Irish Literary Theatre. *Photo Municipal Gallery of Modern Art, Dublin.*

59 TULIRA CASTLE, Gort, County Galway. *Photo Irish Tourist Board.*

60 'LAKE AT COOLE'. Watercolour (1900) by Jack B. Yeats. *Photo courtesy the Victor Waddington Gallery.* ['The Wild Swans at Coole', I, 1–4.]

LADY AUGUSTA GREGORY AND YEATS at Coole Park. *Photo courtesy Major Richard Gregory.* [*Autobiographies, 463.*]

61 THE 'AUTOGRAPH TREE' at Coole Park, Gort, County Galway. *Photo Irish Tourist Board.*

SIR WILLIAM AND LADY GREGORY, Coole Park, 1888. *Photo courtesy Major Richard Gregory.* [*Diary.*]

63 GEORGE MOORE (1852–1933). Painting by Sir William Rothenstein. The author of *Esther Waters* (1894) and other novels, Moore recorded his association with the Irish literary revival in his autobiography, *Hail and Farewell*, which is one of his best works and is an invaluable account of the leading figures in the movement. It was published in three volumes: *Ave* (1911), *Salve* (1912) and *Vale* (1914). Moore was the cousin of Edward Martyn. *Photo National Gallery of Ireland.*

64 ARTHUR GRIFFITH (1872–1922). Griffith, the Irish politician and journalist, began his working life as a printer and became involved in Irish politics after Parnell's fall from power in 1890. He joined the Gaelic League and the Irish Republican Brotherhood (or Fenian Society), from which he resigned in 1906, having founded the Sinn Féin party in the previous year. He founded the *United Irishman* in 1899, and edited it until 1906. Elected the first president of the Irish Free State in 1922, he died before the assembly of its first parliament could take place. *Photo Radio Times Hulton Picture Library.*

65 'MR W. B. YEATS PRESENTING MR GEORGE MOORE TO THE QUEEN OF THE FAIRIES'. Cartoon by Sir Max Beerbohm. *Photo Municipal Gallery of Modern Art, Dublin.*

66 ANNIE ELIZABETH FREDERICKA HORNIMAN (1860–1937). Apart from her association with the Irish theatre, Miss Horniman is chiefly important for her support, from 1907 until 1921, of the repertory company which Sir Barry Jackson directed at the Gaiety Theatre (which Miss Horniman bought and refitted for the company) in Manchester. *Photo courtesy the Mander and Mitchenson Theatre Collection.*

'CATHLEEN NI HOULIHAN'. Scene from the first production in Dublin, 1902. *Photo courtesy the Mander and Mitchenson Theatre Collection.*

67 LADY GREGORY. Cartoon by Grace Plunkett. From Grace Plunkett's *To Hold as 'twere.* British Museum, Department of Printed Books. *Photo courtesy the Dundalgan Press.*

68 'THE KING'S THRESHOLD'. Design by Charles Ricketts for one of the costumes. *Photo Victoria and Albert Museum.*

THE OLD ABBEY THEATRE, DUBLIN. The theatre, destroyed by fire in 1951, was rebuilt in 1966. *Photo Irish Tourist Board.*

69 SIR HUGH LANE, J.M. SYNGE, YEATS AND LADY GREGORY. Drawing by Sir William Orpen. For information about Sir Hugh Lane, see the caption to 'Homage to Sir Hugh Lane' (page 112). *Photo National Portrait Gallery, London.*

70 ABBEY THEATRE PROGRAMME.

71 WILLIAM FAY. Painting by John Butler Yeats. *Photo Municipal Gallery of Modern Art, Dublin.*

'CATHLEEN NI HOULIHAN', performed by the Abbey Theatre Company. Drawing by Ben Bay. *Photo National Library of Ireland.*

72 STÉPHANE MALLARMÉ. *Photo Radio Times Hulton Picture Library.*

73 PAUL VERLAINE. *Photo Mansell Collection.*

74 MONTMARTRE, Paris, during the 1890s. *Photo Radio Times Hulton Picture Library.*

75 J.M. SYNGE. Photograph taken on 31 December 1895. *Photo courtesy Miss Lily M. Stephens.* ['The Municipal Gallery Revisited', VI, 2–5.]

THE ARAN ISLANDS, County Galway. *Photo National Library of Ireland.*

76 'THE PLAYBOY OF THE WESTERN WORLD', performed at the Abbey Theatre. *Photo National Library of Ireland.*

77 YEATS addressing the audience from the stage of the Abbey Theatre. Cartoon by Tom Lalor. *Photo National Library of Ireland.*

'THE AMATEUR CHUCKER-OUT'. Cartoon by Sir William Orpen, from the pamphlet *The Abbey Row* (1907). This pamphlet, which was published by a group of Dubliners, satirizes the uproar which attended the first performances of J.M. Synge's *The Playboy of the Western World*. For information about Sir Hugh Lane, see the caption to 'Homage to Sir Hugh Lane (page 112). British Museum, Department of Printed Books. *Photo R.B. Fleming and Co. Ltd.*

78 YEATS. Caricature (1915) by Edmund Dulac. Best known for his work as an illustrator of books, Dulac also designed the masks and costumes for *At the Hawk's Well*, the first of Yeats' *Plays for Dancers*. Yeats was to dedicate *The Winding Stair and other Poems* to Dulac. *Photo National Gallery of Ireland.*

79 LENNOX ROBINSON. Drawing (1921) by Sir William Rothenstein. *Photo Mansell Collection.*

80–81 'THE WILD SWANS AT COOLE'. Parts of two drafts by Yeats. *Photos National Library of Ireland.*

82 WOBURN BUILDINGS: room occupied by Yeats. *Photo Eileen Tweedy.*

83 THE LIBRARY, Coole Park. A sketch by Yeats. *Photo National Gallery of Ireland. Collection Senator M. Yeats.* [Lady Augusta Gregory, *Coole*, 2.]

85 'EASTER 1916'. Parts of a draft by Yeats. *Photo National Library of Ireland.*

86 THE COUNTESS MARKIEVICZ and a friend on horseback. *Photo courtesy Miss Gabrielle Gore-Booth.* ['On a Political Prisoner', III.]

THE COUNTESS MARKIEVICZ in the cellar of Liberty Hall, Dublin, Easter 1916. *Photo Mansell Collection.*

87 LISSADELL HOUSE, County Sligo. *Photos courtesy Miss Gabrielle Gore-Booth.* ['In Memory of Eva Gore-Booth and Con Markievicz', 1–2.]

LIBERTY HALL, Dublin, after it had been bombarded. *Photo Mansell Collection.*

88 O'CONNELL STREET, DUBLIN. *Photo National Library of Ireland.*

CÚ CHULAINN. Statue in the General Post Office, Dublin. *Photo Irish Tourist Board.*

89 MAJOR JOHN MACBRIDE. *Photo National Library of Ireland.*

90 ISEULT STUART (formerly Gonne). Painting by AE. *Photo National Gallery of Ireland.*

MAUD MACBRIDE (*née* Gonne) visiting women on hunger strike in Mountjoy Prison, Dublin. *Photo Radio Times Hulton Picture Library.*

91 GEORGE HYDE-LEES.

92 YEATS AND HIS WIFE FISHING. Sketch by John Butler Yeats in a letter to Yeats dated 13 April 1918.

93 'THOOR BALLYLEE', Gort, County Galway. *Photo Irish Tourist Board.* ['Meditations in Time of Civil War', II, 'My House', 1–10.]

STONE at 'Thoor Ballylee'. *Photo Irish Tourist Board.*

94 YEATS with his two children, Anne and Michael. *Photo courtesy Shotaro Oshima, author of 'Yeats and Japan', Yeats Society of Japan.*

95 MERRION SQUARE, Dublin. *Photo Irish Tourist Board.*

96 THE GATE THEATRE, Dublin. *Photo Irish Tourist Board.*

97 YEATS at a garden party given by Oliver St John Gogarty, 1923. *Photo courtesy Oliver St John Gogarty.*

98 YEATS. Photograph taken in 1923. *Photo Radio Times Hulton Picture Library.*

99 THE AWARD OF THE NOBEL PRIZE TO YEATS, 1923. *Photo courtesy Nobel Stiftelsen, Stockholm.*

100 SEAN O'CASEY (1884–1964). O'Casey remains probably the most important Irish dramatist since Synge. His reputation rests mainly on his early plays, set in the Dublin slums: *Juno and the Paycock* (1925), *The Shadow of a Gunman* (1925) and *The Plough and the Stars* (1926). His later plays were experimental in technique; the first of them, *The Silver Tassie* (1928), caused the severence of O'Casey's association with the Abbey Theatre. *Photo Radio Times Hulton Picture Library.*

101 'SAILING TO BYZANTIUM'. Part of a proof with Yeats' corrections. *Photo National Library of Ireland.*

102 EZRA POUND. Photograph taken in Pound's studio, 1923. [Letter to Lady Gregory, dated 3 January 1913.]

103 'TWO PLAYS FOR DANCERS'. The title-page of the first edition (1919).

104 THE AVENUE, Coole Park. *Photo Irish Tourist Board.* ['In the Seven Woods', 1–3.]

105 LADY GREGORY in old age. *Photo Mansell Collection.* ['The Municipal Gallery Revisited', IV, 6–8.]

Notes

106 'RIVERSDALE', Rathfarnham, near Dublin. *Photo courtesy Shotaro Oshima, author of 'Yeats and Japan', Yeats Society of Japan.*

107 YEATS. Photograph taken in 1930. *Photo Radio Times Hulton Picture Library.*

108 ETHEL MANNIN. *Photo Mansell Collection.*

OLIVER ST JOHN GOGARTY (1878–1957). Irish poet, novelist and physician, Gogarty is perhaps best known for his entertaining volumes of memoirs, notably *As I was Going down Sackville Street* (1937). *Photo courtesy Oliver St John Gogarty.*

109 EDITH AND OSBERT SITWELL. *Photo Radio Times Hulton Picture Library.*

111 MAJOR ROBERT GREGORY. Painting by Charles Shannon. *Photo Municipal Gallery of Modern Art, Dublin.*

'AN IRISH AIRMAN FORESEES HIS DEATH'. Yeats' manuscript. *Photo National Library of Ireland.*

112 'HOMAGE TO SIR HUGH LANE'. Painting by J. Keating. *Photo Municipal Gallery of Modern Art, Dublin.*

114–115 BEN BULBEN, County Sligo. *Photo Edwin Smith.* ['Towards Break of Day', II, 1–5.]

116 LOUGH GILL AND THE LAKE ISLAND OF INNISFREE, County Sligo. *Photo Edwin Smith.* ['The Lake Isle of Innisfree', I.]

117 KNOCKNAREA, County Sligo. Drawing (*c.* 1833) by John Wynne. *Photo courtesy Lieutenant-Colonel O. P. Wagstaff.* ['The Hosting of the Sidhe', 1–4.]

119 YEATS. Photograph taken during his last years. *Photo courtesy the Mander and Mitchenson Theatre Collection.*

120 MRS PATRICK CAMPBELL in the title part of *Deirdre*, 1908. *Photo courtesy the Mander and Mitchenson Theatre Collection.*

121 PALMA. The harbour. *Photo Radio Times Hulton Picture Library.*

122 YEATS GIVING A BROADCAST. *Photo courtesy B.B.C.*

123 ROQUEBRUNE, Alpes Maritimes, France. *Photo French Government Tourist Office.*

124 YEATS' COFFIN outside the Chapel of St Pancrace, Roquebrune. *Photo Radio Times Hulton Picture Library.*

125 THE INTERMENT OF YEATS' COFFIN at Drumcliff, County Sligo, 1948. *Photo Radio Times Hulton Picture Library.*

YEATS' GRAVE at Drumcliff. *Photo Irish Tourist Board.*

126 YEATS. Portrait bust by Albert Power. *Photo National Gallery of Ireland.*

128 THE CHURCHYARD AT DRUMCLIFF. *Photo Edwin Smith.*

ACKNOWLEDGMENTS

The excerpts from W. B. Yeats' poems quoted in this book have all been taken from *The Collected Poems of W.B. Yeats*, second edition, with later poems added (1950). These excerpts have been quoted by kind permission of Mr Michael Yeats and Macmillan and Company, London and New York, as also have the following extracts from W. B. Yeats' prose writings, quoted on the pages indicated: *Autobiographies* (8, 17–18, 38, 60); *The Letters of W.B. Yeats*, edited by Allan Wade (36, 40, 63, 101, 102, 103, 105, 120, 122).

INDEX

Figures in italic type refer to illustrations